Banking on Believing

A spiritual journey

By Douglas Snowsell

With an introduction by
Preston Manning

Library and Archives Canada Cataloguing in Publication

Snowsell, Douglas, 1943-
Banking on believing : a spiritual journey / Douglas Snowsell.

ISBN 978-0-9878738-2-8

1. Snowsell, Douglas, 1943-.
2. Converts--Biography.
3. Bankers--Biography. I. Title.

BL639.S66 2012 204'.2 C2012-903067-8

Publisher/Distributor
Diamond River Books
Shawnigan Lake.
British Columbia. Canada.
www.DiamondRiver.ca

Interior Illustrations drawn by Barbara Krimmer
Cover Design: Media by Design
www.mediabydesign.ca

INTRODUCTION

In the heart of every human being there is a longing to be intimately known and intimately loved—the longing for relationship. Our true life stories—not the ones we sometimes fabricate to impress others—are largely the stories of our search to satisfy these longings. In this book, Doug Snowsell shares his story—from a boyhood largely devoid of spiritual direction, to a career in banking, to responding to the call of Jesus Christ to "follow him". Doug's experience is that the longing for relationship is ultimately satisfied in a personal relationship with God through Jesus—a relationship which in turn transforms our personal lives, our vocations, and our relations with others. It is an old, old story—yet one that is infinitely varied and fresh when told by someone who has actually lived it. Doug's story will inspire and instruct you. It is well worth reading and sharing with others—especially those who are still searching for relationships that give meaning and purpose to life.

Preston Manning

Contents

Dedication

To my family:
This is really our story.
Thank you all for being in my life.

CHILDHOOD AND YOUTH

The Tractor

"Let out the clutch, Doug! Let out the clutch, damn it!"

My Dad's intemperate words slashed viciously at my ears. They were as persistent as the branches that lashed at me as I ducked down while the tractor careened down the hill.

Our Ferguson tractor wasn't much more than a garden tractor by today's standards but it was more than adequate for our Okanagan apple orchard. It was a simple piece of machinery; something that anybody could operate. At least that is what my father must have thought when he let me drive it.

I was six, and to be invited to work with the men was huge. I don't think I understood ego, but my tiny chest puffed up like our rooster's, and my Dad's confidence in me removed any doubts I had as to whether I could do the job.

I had to drive the tractor between the rows of apple trees so the men could pitch the pruned limbs and logs into the trailer.

One of the main jobs in an orchard is done in the winter when the trees are pruned and if necessary replaced. Once the snow is gone and the ground is dry, the wood and brush are removed from the orchard. I was too small to load logs onto a trailer but Dad thought I was big enough to drive the tractor that pulled the trailer.

Our orchard consisted mainly of mature Macintosh apple trees. Their size meant they were well spaced, and there was nearly 30 feet between trees. They were excellent trees; from one tree we regularly harvested over 400 boxes of apples.

The men started work early. I was so excited that morning I didn't need help getting up.

I sat at the breakfast table with the men. I wasn't slighted that my coffee was seven parts milk. I was one of the men.

It was very cold outside when I went with my Dad to the barn to hook up the tractor. I was deliriously happy and could barely wait for that magic moment when he asked me to jump up and drive.

"OK son, let's get working. You have to drive slowly down the centre of each row and stop if we need more time to put on the wood." No problem, I thought. The Ferguson was easy to operate. A simple toggle switch turned on the ignition and an engine crank started it. Of course I couldn't start it myself but I had watched and learned. Hand cranking was not as easy as it looked. If you didn't do it just right then the engine would recoil and result in a serious injury. My Dad always muttered special incantations to the tractor.

Once the engine started, the clutch and the brake came into play. They were located on either side of the seat housing. I could just reach them by standing up. The gears were operated by a small vertical shifter between my knees on the same housing.

The tractor had four forward gears and one reverse. I put the clutch in and engaged first gear. I moved ahead by adjusting the speed with the throttle lever beneath the steering wheel. The trick was to get up a little speed, engage the clutch again, reduce the revs via the lever and then shift to the next gear. This process got me into third gear. It is more easily done than described. I didn't have much trouble.

After about thirty minutes, I discovered it was not as easy as I had originally thought. I stopped because the men asked me to and then started again in first gear. I tried to shift into second gear and had trouble before I found that gear—it seemed to have disappeared—then the tractor had stopped so I had to start again in first gear. Fortunately we were on level ground.

I was sure the men thought me an idiot for not being able to change gears. My ears were beet red and my confidence flagged just when I needed it most.

At the top end of our orchard the ground sloped up quite steeply. The row of trees ended and I had to make an abrupt turn to go down the next row of trees. The little tractor really could do the job. The grade didn't even phase it even though the trailer had been loaded with a lot of heavy apple wood. The engine didn't seem to work any harder as we climbed.

No one was yet thinking of unloading the wood for stacking and cutting into firewood, but even I could sense the trailer was far from empty.

I climbed the incline, reached the end of the row and turned. I was pleased at my driving success and hoped the hard-working men had forgotten my earlier troubles with the gear box.

Dad was a quiet man. He did not chat idly, but he did have a temper.

As I made the turn, I got the tractor and trailer centred in the middle of the trees on the downhill slope. With the tractor in gear things were fine, but when my Dad hollered, "Slow down." The results were catastrophic. I stood up to push down on the clutch and the brake pedal but gravity pitted the weight of the logs in the trailer against my tiny weight on the clutch and the brake.

The tractor was out of gear but wouldn't stop. I panicked. Dad had said slow down. I had done what I thought was right but it didn't slow down. It accelerated. I had never heard of a roller-coaster but I was on one. I had made a slow controlled ride to the top but now as I hurtled down between the rows of trees, I was on a wild ride. My Dad hollered, "Let the clutch out." His words were useless. I could hear his anger and just panicked and froze. The branches came at me faster and faster. I really don't remember much about that terrible ride.

"Let out the clutch, Doug! Let out the clutch, damn it!" He kept yelling.

The tractor swerved inexorably towards a big tree at the bottom of the run. I could not stop the tractor but it stopped abruptly against a mature apple tree. Steam poured from the damaged radiator and spewed into the cold morning. I was unhurt. I walked half a mile home with tears flowing down my cheeks. I had failed. I was not a man. I was just a boy.

My Early Years

While Dad was serving overseas in the Second World War, Mom and I lived with her parents on their ranch in Glenmore. The house still exists. It then had a wraparound veranda and a gorgeous panorama of orchards and a view of mountains in the distance. Granny's garden was legendary.

Of the few early childhood memories my first real memory was being doubled on my Aunt Di's bicycle down the long driveway. I must have been three at the time. I sat on the seat and she rode the pedals. My aunt was more like my older sister, just five years my senior. We set out down the driveway to the main road about a kilometer distance. The ride was very short. Bloodied and screaming we returned to the house. I was too young to know enough to keep my bare heels out of the spokes—thus my vivid memory!

My Dad did not immediately come home at the end of the war. He had spent years in a German prisoner of war camp and contracted tuberculosis. So before he was repatriated he recovered in a sanitarium in England.

When he came home we moved into a house that was really a picker shack near Uncle Jack's, Dad's brother. I was intrigued by a trap door in the kitchen that led to the cellar. We stayed only one winter. It was a very cold house with no insulation.

We then moved into the Pearson place. Many of the properties were known by the names of original or previous owners. This house was huge and had two full stories. It became a work in progress as we put a basement under the house while we lived there.

Dad seemed to need to make up for lost time and threw himself into the work on the farm. On a typical day his work began at 6AM when he got up and changed the sprinklers in the orchard. Then he made sure that all the animals were fed and watered. We then gathered in the kitchen for a huge breakfast where Dad announced the work plans for the day. I was self-centred and not really concerned with how hard Dad worked but he seemed to work all the time. He worked from sunup to sunset. We rarely saw him during the day. I think he resented the years he'd spent in the war while those who'd stayed behind had prospered. This spurred him on to work harder but it took a few years for the results to show.

We had little family life and no down time. I only remember one time when Dad decided to take us on a vacation.

We went to a dude ranch in the Caribou country near Williams Lake. We were excited at the thought of riding horses, of fishing and making campfires. Just as my brother and I settled in to have some fun, and well before the time to return, my Dad couldn't stand to be away and we went home. It was a non-vacation.

We didn't have much cash but I didn't think of us as poor. We referred to ourselves as orchardists but we also kept a small mixed farm that included chickens, a cow, a calf, pigs and a large vegetable garden. We always ate well.

The Pearson house would be my home until I left to go to university. In spite of the tragedy of losing my Dad there, it was the house I still remember most fondly. On a farm everyone has to work. From when I was very young, I did chores. I fed the chickens and collected their eggs. I was so small I was afraid to stick my hand under the chickens for fear they might peck me. Our geese were also a danger. If the geese were out I had to carry a stick with me when I went from the house to the barn. Animals were either threatened by me or took advantage of my size. The gander was only protecting his flock but his powerful wings could give quite a thrashing, so I was right to be fearful.

We had pigs and a cow for milk. We purchased the cow just before she gave birth to a calf so within the year we had a winter supply of meat. Dad did his best to find time to teach me about my chores and the farm. He taught me to milk the cow. The cow didn't show much respect for a little seven-year-old boy. I remember going into her stall unaware that the cow was very protective of her calf. She butted me hard. My Dad was there in an instant and plucked me out before she could butt me again!

We always had a milk cow. We had more milk than a family of four could use and churned copious amounts of butter by hand. We separated the cream from the milk—there was no homogenized milk back then. The cream went into a glass jar which held about three quarts and I turned the paddles inside the jar with the crank. I turned and churned, churned and turned until the mixture solidified into butter and left a thin liquid known as butter milk.

I recently asked my grandson where milk came from and he had no idea. I told him it came from cows and he thought I was pulling his leg. "No way, Grandpa." I still recall Dad's words as he taught me how to milk the cow. "Gently but firmly grasp the teats and squeeze until a thin stream of warm milk splashes into the can."

Our close cousins had horses. The youngest was younger than me but rode a horse like she had been born on it. She rode over one day and asked if I would like a turn. I was terrified but too conceited to admit it. "Sure," I said and went to climb on. "Not from that side," she admonished and deflated my bravado. I got on and headed into the orchard but I'd been too arrogant to listen to her advice about how to kick with your heels to get the horse to move and how to pull the reins to stop or turn. It just sounded too easy.

I'm sure that horse hated me. She would not go. I kicked with my heels until I felt sorry for the beast. I finally persuaded her to walk into the orchard and actually enjoyed her slow walking motion. When I had had enough, I turned toward my brother and cousin at the barn. As I turned, that horse transformed into a devil. She quickly went into a full gallop. I had no idea how to cope. There was air between my behind and the horse and I was afraid I was going to come off but I clung to the saddle. The infernal beast galloped under low branches and made sure I came off. I made a full summersault off the back and landed amidst my crushed pride. The horse cantered back to my brother and cousin who erupted in laughter. I have hated horses since that day.

I learned how to pick fruit, how to prune and how to thin. I learned how to use and mix pesticides and wonder now how I survived. In those days we spread DDT, a toxic powder now prohibited, with our hands. We used a systemic poison to paint and protect the young root stalks. I nearly blacked out from the fumes even though I worked outside. Perhaps the most radical memory, one that would cause people alarm today, was the sight of one of our workers spraying the poison malathion. He drove down a row of trees pulling the Swanson mist sprayer. It created a halo of malignant mist some 20 feet high. He was encompassed by a billow of spray as he calmly drove the tractor smoking a roll your own cigarette.

In the fall I helped with canning. I was not tall enough to reach the canning machine and stood on an apple box. Yet I learned how to count to fifty-two turns to the right as the machine began to attach a tin top to the tin can. At fifty-two I changed direction and counted again to fifty-two. Why fifty-two? I have no idea, but it put on the lid and made my shoulder muscles burn.

Our winter basement was lined with canned cherries, peaches, raspberries and more. There were jars of mouthwatering dill pickles, sweet and mustard pickles and pickled beets. There were also forty-five gallon drums full of sand that held carrots and beets as well as sacks of potatoes from our garden.

We stored boxes and boxes of apples. Macintosh apples had to be eaten first because they didn't keep very well, while Spartans and wine saps would not be eaten until after Christmas.

The root cellar had a dirt floor, no windows and a single dim light bulb. I hated going to the storage room. I had to face my fear of the dark. I walked anxiously down the narrow stairs with all my senses at full alert. Sometimes my body hair stood on end. I imagined someone rushing out of the dark and hurting me. In contrast I would willingly go out to the barn at night without a light or walk home in the dark. But I still remember the fear I felt in the cellar of that old house.

I have to acknowledge a darker side of my father. He was intolerant, impatient and frequently angry.

I was a shy boy. I remember when I first felt fearful of him. I was five or six and we drove into town. Dad stopped the car up at the local Dairy Queen and said, "Ice creams all round." Then he handed me some money and said, "You pay for them." I was terrified. He shamed me into paying because I was afraid of him.

I am not sure why I was afraid of him but I think it was his temper. Nothing I did satisfied him. I tried to be a perfectionist and escape his disapproval. If I helped him with a repair, he expected me to know the tools he needed. "Not that wrench. I want a three quarter inch one." Even when I gave him the appropriate tool he would swear and ask for something different. I didn't think him unfair or unreasonable at the time—it was just Dad being normal.

One time he tried to teach me how to skip rope. I needed the skill for a Cub badge and I wasn't getting it. Another time he tried to teach me math. He was good at math and had been trained as a navigator and bombardier in the air force. I had trouble just adding. So he decided to teach me. His lesson time was in the evening just before bedtime after he had completed his own chores. We were in the kitchen in front of a blackboard for the math and in the same place for the skipping.

I didn't get it. I either stumbled over the rope or stumbled with the math. Soon he raised his voice. "What's wrong with you? Are you stupid? Try again you dummy. You are not going to bed until you get it right."

I vividly remember my mother who held one end of the rope as they turned it. She was silent for she was also scared of his temper. I was blinded by tears and couldn't see the rope or anticipate the rhythm. I only know the rope thrashed my legs. That didn't hurt as much as the verbal thrashing from my father. I can skip today, but his lessons didn't help.

I never did recover from his math lessons and still think of myself as a math retard. Dad wrote numbers on the blackboard. What is the sum of that? How much is this less that? My mind went blank. I don't know if I feared a blow which never came or the disapproval which came in a flood. We didn't finish any math lesson until after midnight.

None-the-less, I thought of my father as a hero at the time and would often go up to the attic store room, find his uniform and put it on. My Dad was a war hero!

Most of my early years were fun. In the summer we spent weekends at my grandparent's cabin located at McKinley's landing. Granddad

Moubray had died when I was six but the family kept the cabin on Okanagan Lake. I learned to swim, to row a boat, to fish and to hunt for crayfish. I explored a mine shaft that had been left by an optimistic miner who thought he might find gold.

I learned from my Aunt Di there were special stones called flints and agates on this beach. She and I were raised like brother and sister and we would go and sit for hours sifting and turning pebbles looking for these glistening treasures. Parts of these beaches had been used by Indians to fashion arrowheads. She said it was best to search for agate and flints in the early morning when the sun was still low, "then they have a special shine and are smooth to the touch. They also have a different weight and after a storm when waves tumble on the beach they come to the surface." For me anytime was a good time to sit alone on the beach and enjoy the warm sun and the sound of the lake. I was becoming a loner. On these beaches in the past the interior tribes traded furs for flint to make arrows heads. To cut down the weight for the return trip they made the flints into arrowheads and thus I often found shards of flint and agate and occasionally a fragment of a 'worked stone.' These were arrowheads that fractured in the making and were then discarded. On rare occasions I would find a perfect arrowhead that had been inadvertently dropped.

School Years

My first day of school included many firsts. I was in first grade, it was my first day, it was my first time on a bus, and it was my first time in the city by myself. The Kelowna elementary school was a two-story red brick building that we could only enter by one set of stairs. The first time I went up those stairs I was nervous. There were so many new faces and most of them were older and bigger than me. I was insecure. I sat on a small chair with other children, most of them were total strangers, and looked up at a large strange adult who introduced herself as Miss so and so. She was our teacher.

Soon we were sent into the schoolyard for recess. The yard seemed huge. I was used to fruit trees, pine and cedar trees and the big old weeping willow in our front yard but nothing prepared me for majestic chestnut trees and other exotic trees.

When fall came I learned about shiny chestnuts. They seemed to be more important than money. You could throw them at people or you could drill holes in them and make bolos.

I didn't let my timidity show but I was scared of the bigger kids and kept to myself a lot that year. Cecilia was an exception. I sat next to her in class and caused a stir by openly holding her hand. She was my first girlfriend.

The first year went by like a bad dream. Each morning I would steel myself for the bus ride to school and never got over the intimidation I felt going inside that brick monster.

In grade two I moved to a newly built local school in Glenmore. There were still lots of kids, but most were from the Glenmore area and from the same farm background. My teacher was Mr. Brown. He may also have been the principal. I enjoyed school and found it easy.

I still rode the bus and I was introduced to what is today called bullying. We thought of it as teasing. Greta R. comes to mind. Greta's parents were recent immigrants from Germany and unfortunately she often came to school dressed rather distinctly. Her long wool stockings and funny hats stood out and that was an invitation to be teased. Of course I didn't know it was bullying until years later. I would feign sitting next to her on the bus and then flee to another seat saying "cooties".

Someone would snatch her lunch kit and a game of keep away would follow. I do remember that our "teasing" occasionally ended with her crying. Sixty years later at our 50th graduating class reunion I ran into her and she still bore the scars.

When I was twelve I joined the local Scout Troop. I was a know-it-all and was confident I knew more than the Scout leader. I maintained my assurance at the expense of others. I rode the fine line between acceptable and criminal behaviour. When I got close to the edge my friends looked up to me. I did things better and faster and maintained my perfectionism.

I was an active adolescent and a bit of an agitator. One summer evening I was bored doing normal things. At each Scout meeting we practiced our skills and we raised the flag before the meeting and lowered it at the closing. I was in charge of the ceremonies that evening.

We practiced our knots and the use of ropes but when I hoisted the troop leader's bicycle up a thirty foot flag pole, and a knot slipped and it fell, my career as a Scout ended. We all laughed at the oval wheels, except for the Scout leader.

In grade seven I graduated to Kelowna Junior high school. It was another huge brick structure but my experience and age meant I was no longer intimidated. I was a 13 year old know-it-all and I acted out my rebellion in school. Studies were easy but teachers, especially male teachers, became a problem. 'Chrome-dome' particularly comes to mind. He was bald, old and probably just about to retire. I made his life miserable. I think he really cared, but my popularity among my peers was more important than respect for my elders. I showed him no consideration and constantly talked and disrupted his teaching. Every time he took me to the principal's office for a well deserved strapping, my status in class rose. I never gave him or the school authorities the satisfaction of crying or showing pain even when my hands became bruised and red. It was always a good show-and-tell back in class.

In grade seven Pat became my first real crush. She was shy but the prettiest thing I had ever seen. I worked up the courage to ask to walk her home. She said 'yes' and I was in love! I didn't care that I'd missed the bus and had a six-mile walk home.

We went to movies on weekends and during a showing of Elvis Presley's *Love Me Tender* I held her hand. She liked that so I put my arm around her and she cuddled into me. That was bliss!

I now realize that Pat was from what were called the other side of the tracks. Her parents were blue collar and lived in a modest house. I often visited them on Saturday afternoons when Pat and I would sit on a sofa and watch TV with the rest of the family. We were wrapped in a blanket to keep us warm and I was sure that Pat's parents never knew that we held hands under the blanket.

In grade eight I had problems with my science teacher. He was a tall skinny man with a mean streak. He had obviously run into a student like me before. He would sneak up behind me and catch me talking or fooling around. He'd grab a firm hold of my ear and stand me up. He often never said anything, but one look from him spoke volumes.

My grades were always good but I felt lucky not to be expelled.

The Jeep

All my life I have wanted to own a convertible. But in reality it was never practical. What would we do with the kids? How good would it be in the winter? In short it wasn't sensible. But once I did, to all intents and purposes, own a convertible.

It was a Willy's Jeep and I loved it. It seemed to have come straight out of a World War II movie. It had a headlight dimmer on the floor and optional starting with a crank in case the starter motor failed. It had a single hand-operated windshield wiper and just the essential gauges, fuel, oil pressure and speedometer. The gauges weren't accurate. I measured the amount of gas in the tank with a stick.

It had four-wheel drive and a two-speed differential. In these early four-wheel drives I had to stop to engage the low-speed differential or to shift into four-wheel drive. The original Jeeps would hardly count as four by fours by today's standards. For example if one wheel was on ice

Douglas in the Willys Jeep

and the other on bare ground you were stuck. All the power would go to the wheel on ice and it would spin freely. It was barely two-wheel drive!

Even so, I could drive the jeep where a two-wheel drive vehicle would not go. I got to the ponds in the winter. I spent time speeding over the ice and skidding. I was lucky I never broke through the ice.

Another delight was to keep the Jeep operating in the winter. I didn't have antifreeze so every time I shut it off I had to drain the radiator. I reached down to the bottom of the radiator, and opened the peacock valve. I often got burned because the radiator water was still hot. I couldn't let it freeze and damage the engine. Sometimes I lit a fire under the block to thaw it out; sometimes it even worked. During the 1950s, the winters in the Okanagan often dipped below zero Fahrenheit and sometimes the temperature dropped to minus forty. My Dad used to say, "It is cold enough out that your pee freezes before it hits the ground."

I remember my frustration on winter mornings as I tried to start the Jeep. If the battery died, I'd attach a trickle charger and wait hours for the battery to re-charge. Once the engine started, I quickly filled the radiator. It was primitive.

I didn't understand the risks I took. Many probably thought I was not playing with a full deck. The jeep was kept in the shelter of our barn. The barn contained our winter hay. An open fire could have spread to the tinder-dry hay and it never occurred to me that the jeep might have caught on fire.

Despite the jeep's drawbacks, I loved the freedom of driving and felt very grown up. I was fourteen when I started driving it. It was the same year my father died. I am sure he would never have allowed me the freedom to drive it.

I will never forget the last time I saw him. His illness started with a simple cold, but got worse. Finally he had to go into hospital.

As he left our house, he looked at me and said, "Don't worry, son. I'll be back." But I never again saw him alive. He died that night.

He was only thirty nine and I was only fourteen. It seemed to me that his death was a tremendous injustice, and inside me surged a hatred for a God whom I wasn't sure existed.

But whenever I drove up our lane towards the main road I felt great. I was independent and grown up. I explored the hills in the back of our farm and took my .22 Remington semi-automatic rifle. I felt like a mighty hunter.

The jeep had a canvas top but I rarely used it. Most of the time I drove around with the windshield flat on the hood. I let the wind blow into my face and stream into my hair.

I remember one summer day taking three friends for a ride into the hills. We were on vacation, I was a little bored and this was an opportunity to show off. Four in a jeep is a full house.

I knew the hills near our place like the back of my hand. There were no roads but I knew where to go and how to get there. I didn't consider trees less than three inches diameter as obstacles. The jeep's front bumper was made of quarter-inch angle iron and a small tree hardly caused a scratch. It was a great vehicle.

Long before the advent of mountain bikes, I drove up steep hills just to see if I could. The grades were often close to 45 degrees. I would engage the low differential and the four-wheel drive and take a little run at the hill to gain some speed. I always went up. The first few times I was a little afraid but as a veteran I gave quite a thrill to a first time rider. I got a warped pleasure as I saw their faces turn white and watched them hold on for dear life.

Jeeps have a narrow wheel base. I knew little about its relevance until it went over lightning fast. We were all thrown out. We were all badly shaken—even me, the seasoned driver! But miraculously no one was even bruised.

The upturned vehicle's wheels spun in the air like a turtle on its back. Steam rose from the bottom of the engine and the air was ripe with gas and burning oil. None of us thought of fire or explosion. We got together on one side of the jeep, did the 'one, two, three' thing and pushed it back over. I continued with the tour to impress on my friends that this was routine and no big deal. Quietly I wondered how I'd explain the broken and twisted windshield to my mother.

I didn't appreciate how lucky we had been.

Mr. Bert Cooper

After my Dad died my Uncle Bert treated me as a son. In fact both Bert and Auntie Nan treated me well.

Uncle Bert taught me some of the things a Dad should teach his son. He taught me to hunt, especially those plentiful pheasants. I would go over with Joe, my Chesapeake retriever, and my shotgun. We would venture into the coulees and our dogs would scare up birds. We always bagged something. One day I winged a bird and I despaired of ever finding him in the deep alfalfa but Joe got the scent and took off. He wasn't trained to retrieve but was bred for it. I gave up on finding that bird but after 20 minutes Joe came back with the pheasant in his mouth; Joe wagged his tail as though saying, "well, what do you think of me now?" I loved my days with my Uncle Bert.

Sometimes my uncle would invite me on a fishing trip. In the mountains around Kelowna there are many lakes full of trout. We would get up very early and drive for what seemed a long

Doug fishing with Uncle Bert

time up a very steep washboard dirt road full of switchbacks. Our favourite place was Postil Lake which also was a reservoir for Kelowna area orchards. My first sight of the lake after the long trip was always the concrete dam that controlled the water for the valley.

We skirted the lake and drove to the fishing lodge where we rented a boat. The first few times we rowed, later we rented small outboard motors. Once we were settled where Uncle Bert thought there would be fish, he showed me how to tie on a fishing lure. He had me hold the rod at just the right angle, and explained what to do if he caught a fish so our lines wouldn't tangle. I didn't really like fishing—except when I caught a fish. I seemed to wait endlessly, untangle my line too many times and it was often cold and damp waiting for the fish to bite. The effort seemed to outweigh the energy we expended and the fish we brought home. But I was lured by getting up early, packing a lunch and spending the day with my Uncle.

Uncle Bert and Auntie Nan also had a spring ritual of making root beer. I had to wait until it had brewed long enough before I was invited to try a bottle. I rode the three miles from our house to theirs on my bike just for a taste. I enjoyed the root beer but it was their relationship that I wanted.

I respected Uncle Bert and admired him. One day he lifted up the rear end of a car by himself. That impressed me. He was a huge man with a large heart. When he died of throat cancer I was very sad and the part of me that needed a male relationship grieved as well.

Baking – a three-day career

My first job off the farm was at McGavin's bakery. I thought I'd get rich on my wage of $2.75 per hour. I worked evenings after school. On my first shift I worked on a packaging machine. The bread was sliced, then bagged and sent along a conveyer belt where I gathered the loaves and placed them on trays. I constantly had to shut off the conveyor so I could gather up bread from floor. I was relocated on my next shift.

The next night I worked at the ovens. I had to load a tray of bread dough into the oven and remove a tray of baked bread. As I put one in I took a tray out. I was supplied with oven mitts that hung on my wrists so I didn't burn myself. I didn't get it. I burned myself so often they sent me home early.

The next night was my final night at the bakery. I had to load bread into a large semi-truck by pushing a loaded dolly into the trailer. It was simple. The loads weren't that heavy but the stacks were taller than me. It seemed the fates were against my time at McGavin's. The night I became a loader it rained. The steep ramp became as slippery as ice. I didn't get more than a few loads into the truck. Most were on the ground beside it, in the mud and rain

I was not surprised when they didn't ask me to work again.

High School

By my last year at high school in Kelowna I adjusted to city life and flew into grade ten. I was invited to the "in" parties and I was of the few to have my own car. Life was great except that I was not really happy. I was still at the stage that I thought I would find happiness as I went along.

My drinking became a serious business. On most weekends I got drunk. I was looking for the fleeting moments of contentment.

Most weekends were drunks. Girls became essential and most of my relationships were conquests with little regard for the girls involved. I had a solid nucleus of friends. They were my gang and I was secure and comfortable with them.

But eventually I fell for a single girl. She was the daughter of a wellknown local doctor and lived in a magnificent house with a large beach front. My new girlfriend and I were both popular and were invited to all the best parties. I fell seriously in love with her for a few years but her family didn't approve of me. Her father offered me a job as their gardener but thankfully his daughter didn't see the lesson about her mixing with the hired help. That job didn't last long.

I did learn what it was like to really fall for another person. For the first time in my life I felt good about myself.

But there were other attractions in the world and my social life started to interfere with high school. I went less and less to school and then broke up with my girlfriend. I felt pretty sad and sought other distractions. I had often visited the pool hall between classes or after school but then I started to skip classes to indulge my interest in pool. Despite my poor attendance record I maintained good grades in most classes. I floundered in French and both science and math gave me some trouble. If I'd been wise I would have memorized formulas and got through that way but I didn't care enough.

I shared an interest in sports cars with my friends. My first car was a bright yellow Austin Healey Sprite. It raised my stock among my fellow students, while my first serious relationship had traumatized me in terms of risking another committed relationship. I did become a serious party animal.

My friends and I found summer houses, borrowed homes of folks on vacation and had our own large picker shack where we often held our own wild parties.

I recall partying at someone's summer cabin when we ran out of beer. It wasn't a problem as the local hotels didn't close until eleven and we had plenty of time to make it to town in my friend's sports car, provided we hurried. I can't think why I didn't die several times on such trips except perhaps that there was a Divine purpose for my life.

My friend and I jumped into his MGB and made it to the hotel before closing. We loaded up the car with cases of beer. Neither of us was of legal drinking age but that didn't concern the hotel.

We each had a beer in hand as we screamed back to the party. On a long straight stretch of unlit country road, we felt a sudden jolt and saw a meteor trail of sparks behind the car. We were too drunk to realize what had happened until a rear wheel passed us before it veered off into an orchard. The car finally stopped and then we searched in the dark to find the wheel. I can't remember how we got it back on, but we did and returned to the party.

The next morning—and it wasn't just the hang over—I didn't feel any joy from the previous night's revelry. My soul seemed to be very empty.

In high school I chanced upon music and the trumpet. Music seemed to open an emotional side of me that I had never experienced before. I spent hours alone practicing and playing the trumpet, sometimes crying, at other times I just felt melancholy.

I learned to play well and joined the school band, the orchestra and the prestigious dance band. I went on two band trips; once by train to Winnipeg and then to Vancouver by bus. It seems that while I was only trying to have fun I ended up in trouble. On the Vancouver trip we stayed at the Acadia dorms at the University of British Columbia (UBC). They were quite old and have since been torn down. I wonder if my antics had a part to play in their demise. The well behaved types went to bed by curfew. It was an invitation to me. Everyone was in bed; their doors were closed and locked, but hanging in the hall were stirrup pump fire extinguishers. To arouse our sleeping colleagues so we could douse them, we pumped water under the doors. At the time it was hilarious—at least for the pumpers. I am not surprised the leaders threatened to send me home. I think my troubles stemmed from my own inner pain and unresolved anger about my Dad.

Some of my friends were musicians and we played for weddings and parties. It just helped my life to become a round of more drinking and more parties.

Several years after Dad passed away my Mom bought a new car. I am not sure how my brother and I talked her into it, but we encouraged her to buy an Impala from the local Chevrolet dealer. So I got to drive a brand new 1962 two-door Impala hard-top convertible. It was a gorgeous light yellow with a white stripe along the side. It was equipped with 327 cubic inch V-8 engine and a huge four-barrel carburetor. This car smoked. My popularity with the local girls went into orbit.

I did eventually graduate high school by cramming three years into five.

I still wanted to go to university to catch up with the friends who had left me behind to finish high school but I could not have given a good reason why. I think it was that so many of my friends, especially the girls, had gone to UBC in Vancouver. During the school year my life in Kelowna was boring. Kelowna was a tourist town that almost shut down in the winter.

When I did finally go to university I roomed with a couple of friends in an off-campus location. I think this was the worst thing I could have done. We had no supervision, no restraints and no guidelines. For me it was an invitation to party and I did that very well. If I'd been graded on my partying, I am sure I would have earned straight A's. Our parties became so well known that sailors from passing ships shared their shore leave with us. Staying off campus largely contributed to my failure. High school had been comparatively easy, as I didn't have to study hard, but when I got to university I discovered that I didn't know how to study properly. I did well in psychology, anthropology and sociology, mainly because I enjoyed these subjects, but I struggled in Spanish and English.

I enrolled twice at UBC, from 1959–1961. But I had no direction and minimal motivation. I knew I was failing so I left during my second year before I was asked. I got so sick before going home for the Christmas break that I was admitted to the university hospital. I was diagnosed with dysentery but suspect it was caused by failing my studies. I was very depressed and my self-esteem hit bottom. I travelled home in the back seat of a friend's car heavily medicated on tincture of opium. My Mom greeted me at the door and asked, "Where are you going to live?" I blanched. I saw no reason not to live at home, but she went on; "I supported you while you were in school. You are no longer in school so you'd better look for your own place."

I was furious at her, but in hindsight it was the best thing she could have done. At the time I was devastated but I had to find a job.

I moved into a basement suite with my friend Damer Dore mainly because I was dating his sister. I hated living in this basement. I hated eating Kraft Dinner but I didn't have car or any money. One of my uncles, who was very concerned about me, asked "What are you going to do?" When he learned I was unsure where to turn, he put in a good word for me and I got a job in a bank. I had no other alternatives, but it turned out to be a good decision.

MY BANKING VOCATION

Kelowna

The job was in the Bank of Commerce. The bank soon amalgamated with the Imperial Bank and is now known as the Canadian Imperial Bank of Commerce (CIBC). This was my career by default. During the first months I didn't take work seriously. I easily mastered the routine tasks and even managed to play a game of pool most days. I had a deprecating attitude to both the job and many of my colleagues. I started as a messenger but within the first year was promoted first to teller then to discount clerk.

As I was promoted, I took more and more notice of how the branch operated. I became aware of the precision and order. As a teller I had to balance my cash each day. Many a time my supervisor came to my aid as I learned about reversions and how to find errors. If I recorded a fifty-one dollar item as fifteen dollars the result was an outage of thirty-six dollars. What I learned was that most reversions are divisible by nine. Attention to detail translated into getting finished on time because in the bank I couldn't go home until everything was balanced.

On one occasion the entire staff watched a junior accountant come in for the first two days of his vacation—unpaid and humiliated—while he tracked down a difference in the bond department. Curiously, I grew to appreciate and respect banking. I inherently respected discipline and authority.

After I had been employed for several months, I learned that the bank made loans to employees at very low interest rates. I needed a car. I made initial enquiries about how to apply for a car loan and learned that all staff loans had to be approved by the manager. That was intimidating but my desire for a vehicle trumped my fear of the boss so I asked for an appointment and was summoned into his office.

I encountered not a tough old banker but rather a father figure who counseled me not to borrow money! Imagine a contemporary banker dissuading an eligible applicant from taking a loan. He authorized a loan but for a good second-hand car. It was for a lot less than I had planned but my regard for the bank increased.

I was not a good teller. The times I balanced on my first try—a sight balance—were far fewer than the times my supervisors came to bail me out so we could all go home. I wondered if I received my promotion to discount clerk because I was a poor teller.

One afternoon I was summoned into the manager's office. Managers in those days were

A traditional bank of the period

highly respected in the community and almost revered by the staff. Personal exchanges between staff and the manager were restricted to a "Merry Christmas" greeting as the manager walked in and out of the staff party. Anxiously I waited outside his office, but it turned out he gave me a very unusual mission. The large bronze shield from the old Commerce Bank had been placed, as a protest, outside the front door of the Premier of British Columbia, W.A.C Bennett, who lived in Kelowna. The manager charged me to retrieve it.

Now I see celestial irony in my visit to retrieve the shield. In a novella written by my son Colin (*The Frollett Homestead*), he compares two different legacies left in the Okanagan by the Snowsells and the Bennetts. My grandmother, Felicia Snowsell, represented the CCF (Co-operative Commonwealth Federation) party and ran against W.A.C Bennett in his first campaign. She narrowly lost that election. Both families are still represented in B.C. and the Okanagan. The Snowsells fought for the rights of the underdog and stood up for social and environmental issues. The Bennetts built dams and roads which until the 1980s were valued more than clean water, fair wages and fresh air. History will never be re-written, but a case could be made for a foreshadowing of future values when, on that summer afternoon in 1963, a bank trainee, Douglas Snowsell, retrieved a symbol of capitalism from Premier Bennett's lawn.

I had been with the bank about a year and

was starting to enjoy the work when I was again summoned into the manager's office. He told me that I was to be transferred to Greenwood, B.C. He said, "Go home, pack and report for duty Monday morning." He gave me a letter of introduction to my new manager and a stipend for food and travel.

I was being tested. Of course I could have refused and wouldn't have lost my job, but the bank was moving me towards management.

Greenwood

I only had a vague idea of Greenwood's location so on Saturday morning I looked it up on a map and then drove there on Sunday. I was very apprehensive and afraid of the unknown, but I had got a good pay raise and a promotion. I had my own car, a growing sense of my independence and optimism for my career.

On Monday morning I got to the bank far too early. I waited outside for a long time before any staff arrived. The new manager was very different from the one I'd known in Kelowna. This manager didn't even live in Greenwood. He lived in Osoyoos where he was developing a peach orchard in preparation for his retirement. I quickly got the impression that as long as I caused him no problems, we'd get along just fine.

Greenwood was a small town of less than two thousand residents. Its economy depended on a saw mill just outside of Greenwood and a plywood mill located thirty miles away in Midway. The community was so small and so close knit that I'm sure half the town knew what I was going to eat for supper before I did.

I had to drive to Midway twice a month with the mill payroll. The bank in Midway was part of the general store and not really a bank at all. On that half-hour drive I contemplated what I'd do if I was ever robbed. I carried about $100,000 in a small tin box and had a small loaded pistol that I didn't even know how to shoot! Luckily I was never robbed or even stopped.

About half the population of Greenwood was Japanese. They were very gentle, friendly people and only years later did I learn that Greenwood had been a Japanese internment camp during the Second World War. It really made me appreciate their hospitality. I enjoyed my time in Greenwood and was quite sad when a year later I accepted another transfer, this time to Golden, B.C.

Golden

Golden was a Wild West town. The road through the Rocky Mountains, called Rogers Pass, connected Alberta with Golden and the rest of B.C. The road had only been completed a few years earlier. Charlie Bell, my new manager, was a frontier character. He knew everyone in town and they all knew him. He was a banker who operated in his own style. His office was a pawn shop. If customers didn't qualify for a traditional bank loan, they'd turn up with their own security. Charlie Bell had an amazing collection of rifles, fishing poles and the like. He had taken these items as collateral since he knew that friendship and trust were the real security in these deals. The bank had long ago decided to leave him where he was, because Charlie Bell had made it known that he would retire in Golden. He was a conundrum, a banking dinosaur, but I admired his humanity.

Golden was a logging town and the principal logging firm was run by a Russian family. I stood outside their workshop one fall day and watched an unforgettable sight. "Big Mary," the owner's wife, carried two sets of winter logging chains, one on each arm, and threw them down on the ground as though they were bed sheets. Then she carefully inspected them before putting them on the logging truck. I held Mary in great respect after that because each set of chains weighed ninety pounds.

On payday the loggers lined up at the wicket of our most buxom teller. They were valuable clients and they all had large cheques but their comments made me blush. The teller wasn't self-conscious; she appeared to relish their ogling eyes and racy comments. Those loggers were never embarrassed.

After cashing their cheques, they'd spend time at the bars in town, and once liquored up, headed off to the nearby town of Donald which had a wild reputation for its community dances. There were never enough women and the men waltzed in pairs, until they had a disagreement and one knocked the other unconscious. These brawls usually ended up outside the hall with all participating, if not as combatants, then urging on the others.

All too soon a year had passed and I was once again on the move. I was sad; I'd made many friends in this remote frontier town. Wikipedia says of Golden:

After the gold rush the region remained important as one of the only land routes possible for any wagon road to connect the Pacific Colony with the rest of British North America, and although proposed as the route of an intercolonial wagon road by Governor Douglas such a route was not built until the construction era of the Canadian Pacific Railway in the 1880s. As Canada's transportation infrastructure increased the route around the Big Bend became the route of the main interprovincial highway, the section of said route from Revelstoke to Golden becoming known as the Big Bend Highway. With the routing of the Trans-Canada Highway through the Rogers Pass in 1962, and the construction of Mica and Revelstoke Dams, most of the former settled area of the Big Bend Country—a few small hamlets and farms, as the area was never heavily populated despite its important early role in the province—is under water, though the name Big Bend Highway remains as a reference to British Columbia Provincial Highway 23. Mica Creek is the only settlement of any size in the region, other than in areas close to Revelstoke and Golden.

Nanaimo

I was excited to be transferred to Nanaimo on Vancouver Island. The branch was new and a showcase for the bank. It was in a prominent downtown location; the walls were partially glass and it had an elevator with an outside view of the city. It was very modern and was a sharp contrast to the stolid weight of most banks.

But my stay in Nanaimo was extremely short. My immediate boss, the accountant, had a Teutonic heritage and I had British roots. I sensed there might be friction and I was right.

I was courting a young Kelowna girl called Ann Pelly. She was studying at UBC. I yearned to spend time with her. I pined for her presence. At night I could see the lights of Vancouver from my apartment, but there was a harsh reality in the cost of ferries and the time it took to travel to Vancouver. Nanaimo became a prison with little possibility of escape.

One evening, after the bank had closed, we were balancing the day's work. The accountant had his feet propped up on the desk as if he were the Kaiser. He watched us at work but didn't offer help or even encourage us.

Suddenly, he flicked an eraser past my ear. I looked up and caught his eye. A look of concern crossed his face as he wondered if he'd over stepped the mark. I walked over, pulled him out of his chair and said, "Don't ever do that again!"

Within two weeks I was promoted and transferred.

Nelson

Nelson was my next promotion. The accountant there didn't give me any preferential treatment, even though he was married to my cousin, but he didn't tell any of the other staff. He taught me a great deal and I felt that I had an inside track. I also realized that the bank had a strategy in the way they moved their trainee managers from branch to branch. As I moved, my old friendships waned and my loyalty to the bank grew.

Life in Nelson

Nelson was the third place I had lived in the Kootenays. It was a very old city and of great historic importance. In 1867, gold and silver were found in the area and Nelson grew quickly amidst the frantic mining activity. Other mining communities sprang up along Kootenay Lake and two railways ran through Nelson. By

1910, Nelson had its own hydro-generating station, street cars, sewer system, and police force. I became enchanted with the town and location.

I developed a great respect for the peace-loving Doukhabors who were embedded in the Kootenays and yet were treated so shoddily by our governments because they were misunderstood. Much later, when I moved to Saskatoon, in Saskatchewan, I explored the area around Blaine Lake where one of the Doukhobor colonies, fleeing from persecution in Russia, arrived at the turn of the century. I felt it was ironic that they were persecuted in Saskatchewan and fled to British Columbia and the Kootenays to retain their religious freedom and communal way of life.

My growing interest was intrigued by the words of a song we later taught our children.

Here we are in Castlegar
Nelson isn't very far
Load dynamite into the car
Going to blow up CPR.

The rich mining history of the area was evident. I explored a ghost town near Silverton where I wandered through ruins, yet the mining office was largely intact and I could almost imagine returning the next day to find it fully operational. There were racks of core samples and blue prints of the tunnels spread out on large tables. None of the windows had been broken. No one had worked this mine for decades. The dates on the plans told the story.

I found it too far to drive to Kelowna every weekend so I joined up for sports. I had always been athletic, even though I was too small for some sports. I played broom ball in a local hockey arena. One season our bank even had a serious team in a league. The first night I played I went all out. Next morning my groin area was so sore I could hardly move. My cousin had to put on my socks and I hobbled for nearly a week.

The next summer I joined a rugby team. We were a serious team and trained regularly, although some of the training was in applying "liquid bandage" at the local pub after the workout. I remember one league game in Cranbrook. I was a cocky 23-year-old and was not impressed with the opposition who looked like out of shape old men.

I was wrong of course; some of them had played in proper leagues and were experienced. I lasted the first half until I was tackled by one of these older, out of shape men. He clothes-line tackled me and put me out of the game.

My romance with Ann became unstoppable. I was so in love that I would drive to the University of B.C. in Vancouver to spend just a few hours with her! It took twelve hours each way if I ignored the speed limit. The road crossed two of the highest summits in the province. Such is love. We planned to get married as soon as she graduated. Meanwhile I stayed in my cousin's spare bedroom while I searched for a suitable home.

I had enjoyed my bachelor life in the Kootenays and I loved my time in Nelson. We watched great hockey with the Nelson Maple Leafs hosting the Trail Smoke Eaters, the Kimberly Dynamiters, The Penticton Vees, The Kelowna Packers, the Kamloops Chiefs and the Vernon Blades. Two of those teams had played internationally and won a world hockey championship.

Ann graduated in April and we were married the same month. For us it was all about love and had little to do with ceremony, although I did pacify my mother-in law by taking confirmation classes in the Anglican Church and pre-marital counselling from the Archdeacon who married us. Ann had been brought up to be a good Anglican all her life while I had had little to do with religion of any kind. After our one and only counseling session the Right Reverend held me back for a private word. He said, “Doug, if you ever mistreat Ann, I will thrash you.”

Now I had a wife, our own home, a new car and my life was good.

The suitable house I found was a shack out back of our landlord’s home. It was raised on stilts so it could stand on the steep slope. In the winter we had a problem of how to keep all the pipes from freezing but learned never to turn the water completely off. So during the winter the taps dripped continuously.

Our home consisted of nearly four rooms. Our

bedroom was off the living room and separated by a curtain. The bed was against one wall and we had just enough room to get in and out of bed.

The kitchen was a galley like those found on a small sailboat and the bathroom was at the end of the galley.

Our "great room," the living room, was so small that I could put my feet on the coffee table in the centre while leaning on the wall. Our first home was really a shack. We had very little, in material terms, but the time Ann and I spent in Nelson was very precious.

Kingsway and Knight

I hoped my next assignment would be even better. We packed our belongings into our VW beetle and moved to Vancouver. I was to work at the Kingsway and Knight branch. This was another show branch but more important than its looks was its staff.

It was a place of excellence. It satisfied my perfectionistic standards.

Mr. Chumka was a superb manager. He had developed a huge clientele and the branch was very profitable. The accountant, Charlie McLean, had worked in the bank's auditing department for many years and had earned the title of "Audit Charlie" because of his demanding yet fair evaluations. Another of his titles was BMO Charlie because he knew every line of the Branch Management Operations from memory.

He taught me well. "Doug, you have a creditable bank career. You can either build on it, or not. Whenever you make a mistake you lose credibility. If you lose too much you cannot lead.

Doug the Accountant

It is best not to make a mistake." That became our standard. No mistakes. Not even little ones and especially not negligent mistakes. Mistakes were not tolerated.

I learned about loyalty both from the manager and the accountant as they interacted with the twenty-one staff in that office. In turn I was loyal to them.

Once I saw a customer give one of my tellers a hard time. I virtually leapt over the counter when I heard his abuse. I summoned the entire authority of my 24 years, strode over and asked, "What seems to be the trouble?" He answered me in the same abusive tone and demanded we cash his cheque. I told him his behaviour was inappropriate and that if he wanted to shout, he should shout at me and I would call the police. He calmed down and we resolved his issue. My stock with the staff rose several points that day.

I also owe a deep debt of gratitude to Stella. She was practically the office manager and one day she realized I had made a serious mistake. She confronted me and I quickly admitted that I'd been wrong. Again my stock went up. Stella was extremely loyal to me and after that she deferred to me as Head of Office.

Each month the branch has to balance all its accounts to what is called a General Ledger (GL).

We had twenty-one thousand savings accounts, several thousand chequing accounts and thousands of business accounts. Each was represented by a card or sheet and every account had to be added and totaled together to arrive at the GL total. There were no computers in those days. I know of no other branch that did what we did that year. Our staff of twenty-one combined their totals and arrived at the right balance, to the penny, the first time. We had made what is called a sight balance. It was stunning. Even Charlie was impressed and perhaps this was the moment he decided I could be trusted with his job. At any rate I was promoted within the office and became the accountant. This office was mine. I was the captain of this ship.

Ambition became my demanding taskmaster. I loved my new job and the authority and recognition I earned really motivated me. I took every course the bank offered and studied at university at night. Ann and my young family didn't appreciate my dedication to my work. To them my life had taken a treacherous turn.

I became a workaholic and often worked ninety hours a week. When I was not working at the office I went golfing with the right people. There was a subtle change in my relationship with customers now that I was the accountant. They sought me out and offered me social invitations. One such invitation taught me a great lesson.

An affluent East Indian business customer solicited my attention and eventually invited me to his home. I had no idea what to expect and confess I entertained considerable racial prejudice at the time. But I was also honoured and proud to accept the invitation.

His home was a new world of smells and sights. He ushered me into his living room. Although there were other people in the house, they didn't join us. He and I were alone in the living room.

He poured us each a generous glass of scotch. Then he served food. I didn't want to appear ignorant and did not ask what the dish was. I think it was a pea flour cake seasoned with poker-hot spices. Each light and fluffy cake was the size of an egg. They looked benign. I popped one in my mouth. My host watched me. First my mouth caught fire, then my eyes wept and finally I thought the top of my head would explode. I grasped my almost full glass of neat scotch and swallowed it like water.

I did feel that my host had set me up and might also have been a racist himself. He poured me more scotch while I tried another pea flour cake, but this time I only took half a piece. Unfortunately, the result was the same and I gulped down my scotch to extinguish the fire in my mouth, throat and belly. I was becoming pretty sloshed from all the scotch so I excused myself and left with some dignity intact. I am haunted by what happened in that house and I am sure I heard laughter as the door closed.

Vancouver Data Centre

I gained a great reputation as the accountant at Kingsway and Knight and was in line for a promotion to a larger branch and a more senior accountant position. Instead I was offered the position of operations manager at the Data Processing Centre. Initially I was unsure about whether to accept this promotion. I would be out of the main flow of banking and there might be less scope for future advancement but I would be on the cutting edge of a new technology. So I accepted and was very glad I did.

In a very short time my salary rocketed. The bank did not expect me, as the manager of the computer technicians, to earn less than they did. And in those days computer technicians were very well paid. My salary doubled within four years.

In 1966 computers were primitive and very

large. The first computers in the data centre were Honeywell 8000s and had vacuum tubes inside them. They generated so much heat that refrigerated air was fed though a 12-inch space under the floor to control their temperature. I had no knowledge of computers, just an encyclopedic knowledge of accounting and banking procedures, so I had a very steep learning curve to understand and integrate accounting procedures with computers. We considered it a great night if the computer did not go down at least once. Vacuum tubes are not reliable!

Those in main line banking knew very little about the operations of the data centre. I didn't deliberately pull the rug over their eyes but quickly realized I was in the driver's seat. Procedures, staff, and equipment that I recommended, I usually got.

I loved my job. I was the leader of a team and loved the people who worked for me. While in Vancouver I helped plan the construction of a modern computer centre and the move of the data centre to a new location. This turned out to be valuable experience in my next position.

SPIRITUAL AWAKENING

Karate

My spiritual awakening began because of my growing dissatisfaction with life. I had been drinking heavily and more than just socially. My workaholic tendencies meant that I was not a good family man. In fact I had difficulty adjusting to becoming a father. I had left family planning to Ann and I was horrified rather than pleased when she announced she was pregnant. We had been living in an adult-only apartment and a child meant we would probably have to leave. In fact when Brandon was born, management turned a blind eye, but when Colin was born just 14 months later, we had to move.

I purchased a modest small bungalow in Surrey. Ann and I maintained a very rocky relationship and I was at the bottom both physically and spiritually. I knew I had to do something to enhance my self-worth and find purpose.

I am not a large man and I suffered from a degree of insecurity. I was never going to develop into the "bully of the beach" but had long been fascinated with martial arts. Once, in my early teens, our farm foreman, Nobee, who held a black belt in Judo, tried to teach me. His lessons didn't last long as I disliked being thrown repeatedly onto the floor!

Karate, however, seemed to be more to my liking. I found an excellent club and developed a great friendship with my teachers and owners, Jim and Judy.

The first time I sparred was with a young man named Mark, who had his green belt. I felt the wind of his feet brush my face and occasionally his light touch. He admonished me to "defend myself." My answer was, "How can I defend against what I can't see?"

But within a year of karate training I began not only to "see" but to react quickly. I also enjoyed the mental discipline and training of karate. I felt as though I was focused on a different philosophy. I retain many pleasant memories of those days.

One summer Saturday afternoon at the club in New Westminster, I was "babysitting" my son Colin. He was about two at the time. We were all training hard and the first-floor windows were open. I was preoccupied and didn't watch Colin closely. I didn't notice him leave the main room and toddle into the change room. He must have found a pair of cowboy boots belonging to another member. I didn't see him bring the boots out to where we were practicing or see him climb up on one of the heat registers to look out the window and throw the boots out the window. I didn't discover his escapade until we were getting dressed. "Where are my boots?" my mystified friend asked. I questioned Colin who was very pleased with himself and almost boasted about what he had done. I had to buy my friend a new pair of boots.

I had many new experiences during my years practicing karate. Once four members of another karate club came to our dojo to challenge us. I remember Jim asking us senior pupils to get ready. The sensei of the opposing club had been denigrating our style and our members. He wanted to demonstrate the superiority of his style and his club. The challenge was very brief and ended when Jim threw their sensei down the stairs. Not a small thing as there were seventy stairs. His body went bump, bump down the stairs and then there was a loud crash when he hit bottom. Then there was silence.

The first open competition our club attended was held at the old Pacific National Exhibition (PNE) building. We had an opportunity to compare our style with the best fighters from across North America. We were all nervous, or at least, I know I was.

Slowly, it became obvious that our fighters were doing well. We won most of our fights. When it was time for my fight, a problem with a rival club came to the forefront. They didn't like losing and were determined to win, whatever the cost. Competition rules stated that blows to the face, groin or legs were forbidden. I stood on the mat and faced my opponent. I bowed and started to fight. Almost immediately I was forcefully struck in the face. The blow broke my nose. I was dizzy and fell down. My nose bled profusely. The referee came over and brusquely asked if I wished to continue. I was a determined young man and said, "Give me a couple of minutes," I got up, nose still bleeding, then faced my opponent again; only this time I understood what it would take to win.

He came in more cautiously than before. I waited for him to move and then countered his advance with a full power body shot. The rules forbade the use of full power but the referee didn't penalize me. My opponent's face contorted in pain but I was awarded the point. When we began again he was even more cautious. I'm sure he still felt the force of my previous blow. My nose continued to bleed and each drop of my blood fuelled my anger. I am sure he sensed and felt my animosity. I didn't wait for his advance but struck first and landed another forceful blow to the body and was awarded the bout.

We never found out our club ranking in that tournament because Jim withdrew our club and protested the lack of rules enforcement. What had happened in my bout was not an exception and several of our fighters had already been hurt. I admired Jim for protecting us.

A doctor tended to me after my fight. He told me, "Blow." I thought, "Are you crazy?" But as he was the doctor, I blew my nose. He confirmed, "Yep it is broken." My nose has looked like the first initial of my last name ever since.

Finding New Life

Since my father's death, I had been consumed with an overbearing hatred of God and religion. This hatred became the dominant emotion in my life. Hatred was destroying me from within. I could not selflessly love, even though I wanted to.

I became a bank manager and directed hundreds of employees. My wife excelled at social functions. We had two good-looking sons and owned two cars, two dogs and a lovely house. We had built it according to our own tastes and I earned a salary that was high enough to pay for our lifestyle.

I believed in certain ideals, that one should love his wife, be a good father and go to church at least at Christmas and Easter. I went to church very seldom but didn't become involved. I felt unable to love my wife and sons the way I should. I tried to soothe my conscience by buying them things, but I could not give them the affection that I did not have. Outwardly, I appeared to be a success, but inside I felt a failure.

I did not want to admit this, even to myself, so I buried myself in activities. I played golf twice a week and attained a blue belt in karate. I studied at university at night and maintained five aquariums of tropical fish.

My pace was relentless, but life did not satisfy me. I drank excessively and even experimented with drugs. If I had been poor, I might have thought money would satisfy me, but my experience had shown that more money, activity and alcohol was not a solution. Elbert Hubbard's quote seems apt.

"Life is just one damned thing after another."

My spiritual awakening took place in March of 1973. One Saturday I felt even more depressed than usual. My woes seemed interminable. My family was not home. Rain had cancelled my golf game. The television was not working and I did not feel like going to a bar. I paced the house seeking an outlet.

Then I saw a book my wife had left on a table. She had surprised me the year before when she said, "I have met Jesus."

I was angry when she told me this; I felt religion was just for women and weak people. I hadn't tried to learn anything about her religious experience. But at that moment I took up the book and read it. It was a collection of testimonies about unhappy people like me who had met Jesus.

Someone, Not Something

Something inside me started to disintegrate as I read about a God who loves, pardons and transforms. My hatred of God lessened while I read. I realized that the reason for living is not found in something, but rather in someone—in Jesus!

I felt unusual feelings within me. As I read I felt concern that I had failed so badly in my relationships. The book told me repeatedly that God loves. I always thought that I was a good man. But in the inspiration of that moment it became unbearable to me that all I should have done, I had not.

I had not loved my sons and had missed too many opportunities to make them happy. I felt condemned because I had rejected God. I understood I was a sinner. My pain was unbearable.

I thought, *O Jesus, if this is the truth, I need You! You are my only hope. Can I meet You like the people in this book have done?*

I threw myself on the floor and cried. Our society holds that it is not proper for a person to do such a thing. But at that moment I was meeting God and He was cleansing my heart.

My sixteen-year hatred slipped away and was replaced by a profound love. Everything appeared new. Jesus came into my life on that day and I know He will never leave me.

In that moment of seeing myself in the light of a holy God and remembering my many years of bad behaviour to those near and dear to me, I realized I desperately needed to be delivered from a life over which I had no control. Slowly, as my new life began to grow, my values changed so that by the summer of 1974 we decided to take a month's vacation. Before this, I had been satisfied with a couple of days here and a long weekend there, but I made no real separation from work life. The first step for us as a family was to go camping for one month.

During that month we explored many areas of British Columbia, especially the Prince George and Fort St John areas. Then we decided to make the trip to Edmonton, Alberta, to visit family. We had a prejudice against the prairies but it melted away as we experienced long warm days and magnificent skies. Our eyes were opened. As we drove back to the coast I said to Ann, on the highway near Hope, "Honey, if God called us I think we could even leave B.C."

These were prophetic words. I'd been back at work just a week when I took a call from the head of the Bank's Data Centre in Calgary. He introduced himself and asked me, "Have you ever considered moving?" My mind moved a hundred miles a nano second as I responded,

"Yes."

"Would you consider moving to Calgary to

run our data centre?"

Without hesitation I replied, "Yes, I will come."

He was silent on the other end of the line for a few moments and then said, "You can't just make a decision like that. You need to come here and see what the job is like."

"I will come," I replied, "but I already know I will take the job."

Calgary Data Centre

I arrived in Calgary in the fall of 1975, only months before the city really began to boom. I immediately immersed myself in my job. My family followed months later. I commuted between the coast and Calgary on a bi-monthly schedule.

I was the administrator of a large data centre for the CIBC and I loved it. My life seemed more balanced. In the eyes of the world I was a success. In my own eyes I had a spiritual life and sound values. I did well and in January 1977 the Data Centre Manager gave me one of the best annual reviews in my 16 years in banking. He confirmed I was still the golden boy.

In March he called me into his office. This was not unusual, as I consulted with him several times a day and often in his office. Once in his office, he could hardly look me in the eye.

He looked at his shoes and said, “Doug, you’re not working out here. I’d like you to request a transfer.” He then added quickly, “We’re not letting you go; you just need to leave this office. Be assured that wherever you wish to go your wish will be granted.” It had been only two months earlier that I had listened to his fulsome praise of my achievements and of my efficiency. He had given me the best annual review of my banking career, so I was incredulous.

Over thirty years later I still find it hard to express what I then felt. His comments blindsided me. I was shocked, hurt, angry, and bewildered. I felt that the bottom had fallen out of my world. I struggled to my feet and, as I left the office, said, “I can’t think right now. I am going home.” He agreed and made no effort to keep me at work.

My bus ride home seemed unusually slow but I felt an almost surreal feeling of calm and security. Between the office and home, I decided that my manager’s request was unjust, unfounded and unacceptable and I decided to submit my resignation. I was sure that an employee as valuable as I had become would never be so unexpectedly let go. I expected an investigation and I was sure justice would prevail. Ann was surprised to see me home so early but I told her we had some important matters to discuss.

I felt peaceful and calm, yet I had no plan. I wondered how I could tell my wife whom I had moved away from her home and support system in B.C. that I was going to resign. Moreover, I had no idea what I would do or how we would live.

I said, "Ann, something happened at the office today that is wrong," and I went on to explain what happened. "I am going to present my letter of resignation tomorrow morning." She was standing in front of me and she had a broad grin plastered on her face. I thought, "She doesn't understand." I recounted the story again, slowly and deliberately and added more detail. Her grin just got wider and deeper. "Doug, this is an answer to my prayer!"

I was confused until she explained how a small group of women friends, all new believers, had read a book titled, *What Happens When Women Pray.* These spiritual novices took the book very seriously and when instructed to divide the pages of a note book into columns entitled, Prayer Request, Date of Request, Date Answered, Details of answer, they had done that. They were full of enthusiasm but wondered, "What do we pray for?" Ann had the answer, "I know that Doug wants to study the Bible but doesn't know how we could manage it. Let's pray that he can go to Bible school!"

I had no clear idea of what was involved in going to Bible College, but knew I wanted to study the Bible and had every intention of returning to a secular life once my studies were completed. Of course I had no idea that the course at the Bible College was four years of study.

I had not wanted to leave my job, leave Calgary or move, especially to Regina, but Regina was the home of the Canadian Bible College-(CBC). The Regina locals always joked. "Regina isn't the end of the world but you can see it clearly from here." But our sovereign God was moving and guiding our lives.

God's hand was evident in our move to Regina. Firstly, I was never asked by the bank why I left. That hurt me, but later I realized it was just evidence that God was in control. Then our realtor found a house purchaser in a matter of hours. We didn't want to move until the end of the school year. That wasn't a problem for the purchaser. We needed the money in advance. Again, that was not a problem for the purchaser. When we met the people who were buying our house, we found out they were retired missionaries and knew the young couple who had been teaching us about the Bible. This was another confirmation that we were being led by God. Finally, when the deal went through we saw that our realtor had taken no commission. He humbly told us, "I didn't sell this house, God did."

My employment in the bank at Calgary lasted only 18 months, but in that time we tripled our real-estate investment.

Two months after we had settled in Regina I received a card from a friend in the Calgary Data Centre. It began, "Did you know?" and told me how the manager on the evening shift was caught embezzling, was tried and was in jail.

The embezzler had wanted me transferred because she knew that I would catch her. The irony was that when I left, as a senior officer of the bank, she ensured that my departure would be followed by a forensic audit. During the audit, the bank inspectors became suspicious then returned unannounced and caught her redhanded.

CBC: Not a Radio Station

I clearly remember the stress of our move to Regina. We felt we were well prepared. The movers took our household contents the day before. We agreed to meet them at our new home in Regina. So, we spent the night at a friend's house. We only had to go to our old house, pick up our dogs and drive to Regina. When we arrived, we discovered the gate had been left open and the dogs were gone. We panicked. We had to leave to get to our new house when the movers arrived, but we couldn't leave without the dogs. We called the dogs but weren't even sure if they could hear us. But then we had inspiration. We decided to pray and ask God. He in His mercy and faithfulness interceded on our behalf and the dogs appeared as if by magic. We started out on the nine hour drive to Regina. It was July 1st 1977.

On our first Sunday in Regina we went to church. We arrived just as the congregation was leaving for a church picnic but they invited us. We felt uncomfortable as we arrived at the local park with nothing to add to the picnic.

Colin was of an age where he wanted to join in but wasn't quite old enough. He quickly made friends with a tall man who played catch with him. Don, as we learned he was called, was extremely patient with Colin.

We chatted and he learned that we'd moved to Regina to attend Bible College. He asked, "How are you going to afford it?" "What a nosy parker," I thought to myself. I simply answered that we would be okay and added, perhaps sanctimoniously, "God will provide."

Whenever we saw Don, which was at least once a week in church, he would inquire, "How are things going? Do you need a job?" After a month when bills arrived and we didn't have the money I finally swallowed my pride and asked what he did for a living. He replied, "I work in construction and apply stucco wire to houses."

I had worked in a bank and knew nothing about construction or about stucco or wire. I didn't like hard physical labour and so once again I told him we would be okay. Although there wasn't a great deal of conviction in my voice.

The next time we met and he inquired I asked, "Tell me what it is that you do again." He explained and said he would teach me all I needed to know. "Don, if you can teach me how to do this, then I'll make you a deal. You teach me stucco wiring and then I'll teach you patience." I implied that he would need patience if he was going to teach me—a novice in any type of construction—how to be a stucco wire technician.

The next day, Don picked me up in an old pickup loaded with ladders. I jumped in enthusiastically. I had great hopes that Don would be the best thing to happen to me in a long while. I was going to earn an income and work with a Christian brother.

I waited expectantly but Don didn't start the truck. Instead he removed his hat and invited me to pray. "Wow," I thought, "This is going to be great!"

"Dear Lord," he began, "We are two of your children who are ready to work and you know that we do not have a job." "What?" I shouted in my mind. "What have I gotten myself into? This guy is nuts." His prayer continued. "Please find us work. In Jesus' name. amen."

We did find a job later that day, but we didn't have to start until the day after. As I look back I think that was the only day in my four years at college that there was no work for us when we wanted to work. In fact during those four years Don's company grew from the two of us and one old beat-up-pickup truck into several crews working out of two school buses and grossing nearly $500,000 per year. I don't know how many college students Don helped but it was many.

I found school hard. I had never learned how to study and my performance at university had been dismal. Towards the end of my first semester I suffered a breakdown. "I can't do this," I thought. "What am I thinking? I am a failure. What have I done to my poor family?"

Ann, who had done well at university, came to my rescue. She consoled me and then taught me how to study. In the first semester my grades were not great but I did manage to pass all subjects. After the first semester my studies became increasingly easier and much more enjoyable.

My studies were my job. I studied hard for seven hours a day. Then I had time to spend with my boys or putter in the yard.

I had wanted to attend Bible School because of how little I knew of the Bible, yet I knew the Bible was key to my being a good husband, a good father and a follower of Christ. Yet, when I met Jesus I didn't even know the Bible comprised both an Old and New Testament!

I was convinced that at the end of four years of Bible School study, I would know all about things biblical. I was hopelessly optimistic and that showed my lack of understanding and my own enormous pride.

Nonetheless, that was why we moved to Regina. We planned to return to B.C. when I finished school, get a regular job and resume our secular life. But as the saying says, "The best laid plans of mice and men oft times go awry."

One morning I was in my study in the basement reading my Bible and spending time with the God I love. He often spoke to me through His Word but that morning I heard His voice as He said, "Doug I don't want you to return to work in the secular world, I want you to work for me."

I bounded upstairs to the bedroom where Ann was spending her own time with God. I rushed in, a little breathless and said, "We are not going back to the bank or the secular world, we're going into the ministry!" "I know." she replied. She had already foreseen it and made a note in her journal. How we praised God.

From that moment on my studies and our time in Regina took on a whole new meaning. I knew I was preparing for something but I did not understand the purpose. In my naïveté I dreamed how I might pastor a church, even a large one. I thought with all my banking experience it would be quite easy.

A Preacher is Born

In my homiletics class at Bible College I was encouraged to seek opportunities to preach. I was invited to speak in a small Lutheran church north of Regina. I prepared a message very carefully and used all the interpretations I had been taught. I arrived early on the Sunday morning to orient myself. I hadn't ever seen the inside of a Lutheran church before. It was quaint. It sat forty people but in other ways it was a cathedral. It had stained-glass windows, carved oak pews and a beautiful pipe organ behind the choir loft high over the front of the church. The pulpit was at the front up a few stairs. It looked like the prow of a ship jutting out in the front of the congregation. I didn't preach from the pulpit but at a stand in the front of the congregation.

The simple service commenced with a church

member opening in prayer and then the congregation would sing a number of hymns. Then I would preach and we would finally finish with one more hymn.

The opening prayer and announcements went perfectly but we didn't immediately sing. We could see the organ loft at the front of the church; but no sound came from the organ. The organist made exaggerated motions at the organ and we realized something was wrong. She signaled with shrugging of shoulders and upheld palms that the organ would not play and she didn't know what to do.

The church was silent. No one took charge but the congregation looked at me. I assumed they didn't want me to try to fix the organ and they didn't look like a group that would relish singing a cappella, so I walked up to the front and started to preach. I gave an enthusiastic performance. When I finished I added a prayer for good measure and sat down. I looked discreetly at my watch and was mortified to see that opening prayer, announcements and preaching had taken just fourteen minutes!

No one else seemed to mind. I think most were pleased to get out of church early and go home.

A Preacher is Proven

I had no experience working in a church, except for my fourteen minutes in the Lutheran church. But for four months during the summer of 1979 I helped the pastor Lloyd Draper, in Kelowna. He was a true friend and mentor.

To work in Kelowna was a dream come true. This was my home! It was summer and Kelowna is one of the best vacation spots in the world. Our boss, Mr. Draper, frequently invited us to leave work early for a swim in Okanagan Lake. He ensured there were drinks and watermelon for all.

I was in Kelowna to learn about the church. When he asked me to preach at the morning service to the congregation of several hundred, many of whom knew me. I was intimidated.

He gave me three weeks to prepare a sermon.

That should have been more than enough time; but for me, three months was not nearly long enough. I used a temporary office in

Douglas, the preacher

the church nursery. I had a table, a telephone

and a carpeted floor. I originally felt honoured, as the senior pastor did not have carpet in his office, but on warmer days I realized the carpet reeked of the little people who played and peed there each Sunday.

Several days before the scheduled sermon, I was at an impasse in my preparation. But my preaching debut inevitably approached. I needed to be filled by the Spirit of God, so I asked. I got down on my knees and beseeched God to fill me. Nothing palpable happened at the time but I got a supernatural confirmation when I preached on Sunday. I was in my chair on the platform waiting to preach. I was sick to my stomach and my knees knocked. When I walked to the pulpit, I heard God's voice, "Just love them, Doug. They are not your enemies." My preparations came alive as if another dimension had been added to my words. I became God's orator. After the service several people compared me to Billy Graham but I knew that God had filled me with his spirit as he must have empowered Billy Graham.

Car miracles

In the years of our ministry God has helped us time and time again with our cars. In the summer of 1978, after our first year in Regina, we drove to B.C. for a two-week holiday that Ann had from her job. We had volunteered to teach in the District Vacation Bible Study (DVBS) at our church in Regina after our holidays. We had started to prepare for it and planned to complete our preparations during our time away.

I remember how we tried to see everyone and do everything, but at the end of two weeks we were exhausted. Ann didn't want to return to the exhausting routine of work and wasn't looking forward to DVBS. We wished we didn't have to return. Ann knew she had responsibilities waiting, but it would have been nice to stay longer in B.C.

The day scheduled for our return to Regina arrived and we left in our VW station wagon. On the freeway out of Vancouver I sensed a car problem. I said, "There's something the matter with the car." I pulled over and crept along the shoulder, I said to Ann, "We've got to get off the freeway." We took the first exit but I had no idea where to drive or what to do. I aimlessly turned left and right until finally, with the car barely crawling along, I saw a VW repair centre! I didn't know where we were, but God did, and He had directed me to make every decision to turn left and right so we arrived at the garage, just as the car died. I never heard his voice or felt any direction, but I had sensed where to turn. I could not say that I been obedient, but as the car seized on the garage forecourt, I knew God had been my guide.

I went in and awaited the mechanic's verdict. He said, "It's a major repair and will take a week." I was actually overjoyed. Ann and I were both exhausted and we suddenly had an extra week.

It was a whole week for Ann to rest. I phoned my aunt in Surrey and let her know—she was overwhelmed that we were thrilled about a car's breakdown. The mechanic estimated the cost at five hundred dollars—a large sum in those days—but all I could think of was "rest". And, Ann and I did rest. Ann didn't have to work at the DVBS, and our friends and relatives in the Vancouver area thought we had gone home; so we rested. God knew it was exactly what we needed.

I even had five hundred dollars; I had saved it for school fees, so after our rest, we paid our engine repair bill and headed home. On the way we stopped in Calgary and went to our church. As we sat in the service, an unmarked envelope was passed to us. We opened it, and inside was—A MIRACLE! It was five hundred dollars!

During that holiday we experienced God's miraculous guidance and God's miraculous provision. It is of tremendous comfort to me that God never changes, and that His miracles guided and provided for us.

The new car miracle

Miracles show us God; miracles encourage us in our belief; miracles can challenge us to believe. Often a miracle does all these things!

During the summer of 1979 God used a miracle in Kelowna to convince Ann's Mom of His existence and power.

I had driven from Regina to Kelowna in our VW station wagon, but as I drove it around Kelowna, I became more and more concerned about its ability to make the trip back to Regina at the end of the summer. Finally, it became obvious that we needed another car. As an intern I didn't earn a salary, and Ann and I would both have to pay tuition in September because Ann would attend seminary in that last year and would have no income. We prayed for a new car and told Granny what we were doing. She looked puzzled and said, "Aren't you going to tell anyone?"

One Sunday I was delighted to see our dear friends Nancy and Dennis from Calgary.

After the service, we joyfully greeted each other and went to lunch at a restaurant. We were pleased to catch up on each other's lives and enjoyed our fellowship. Over coffee, Dennis said, "Doug, the Lord is telling me you need a car." I told him that was the case. I was amazed because I had not broached the subject "Well," said Dennis, "I have a car for sale." *So what?* I thought, *I have no money.*

"I would like to give it to you." continued Dennis, "but that will complicate the transfer papers. So, I'll sell it to you—for one dollar." One dollar! Dennis had mentioned it was a Ford Granada and I was thrilled. Ann didn't know about cars and wasn't nearly as thrilled and appreciative as I was. But later, we went by a used car lot and I showed her a Granada. She saw what a luxurious miracle God had performed! So, the next week Ann, Brandon, Colin and Doug (ABCD) and Granny piled into our little VW and coaxed it back over the Rockies to Calgary. We began to refer to ourselves as the ABCD Snowsells to make it easy for our supporters to remember who we were. Over the next sixteen years it became our "brand."

There we finally said goodbye to our Volkswagen. I gave Dennis a one dollar bill, signed the papers, and drove back to Kelowna in the Grenada. It was a treat. The car had power steering, power brakes, a smooth ride, and was whisper quiet inside. We talked rather than shouted at each other!

Once again, God had miraculously provided and Granny was the witness. At the end of the summer, after she had prayed for Jesus to come into her life, she said, "Well, if I hadn't seen Him and learned about Him this summer, I never would have."

We thought at first that God had been delightfully frivolous in giving us a luxurious vehicle but we later realized He had been very practical.

The following summer we would prepare to go to the mission field. We didn't know that we would be exempt from home service before becoming missionaries. But God did! He foresaw the long trips we would make in the winter, spring and early summer to speak in churches. He knew we would need a reliable car. He also wanted us to have a comfortable car. Every trip in our old Volkswagen we felt like we had pedaled the whole way. More importantly, God gave us a silent car so that our family, ABCD, could drive, talk, sing and pray together—He gave us family times to treasure before our years of separation.

My Call to Missions

The semesters flew as we shared a new sense of purpose and determination to learn all we could to prepare us for a new and exciting future. One morning during the last semester in our third year I heard the same voice speak to me, this time from Ecclesiastes 4:1.* We had recently learned that ninety per cent of Christian workers work with ten per cent of the world's population. How unfair, we thought. We don't want to do that. At the time we had no idea how this would affect us as a family or its significance in our call to missions.

I could have rejoiced to receive a call to work arm in arm with the ten per cent reaching the majority of the world's lost. But I did not rejoice. Ann and I had been in the church stream for long enough to know that we did not qualify as missionary candidates in our church denomination. We did not have either the education or experience. We might have been able to remedy these deficiencies but we had to have all qualifications in place before my 28th birthday; I was already 35.

But God had clearly spoken missions. We started to look for another agency that would sponsor us. Then God stepped in. He had prepared us for this years earlier by bringing the Cook family into our lives. I had become Arnold's close friend and then unbeknown to me he was about to be appointed Vice President of Missions in a newly formed independent Canadian branch of our denomination. He called me and said, "Snowsell, slow down. I have heard you are considering going with another mission. Don't do anything rash. I am not supposed to tell you this," and he then told me of coming changes.

God wanted us in Chile. He arranged for us to be sent as the first Canadian missionaries under the newly formed Canadian branch. We were exceptions to the rules.

Ecclesiastes 4:1 *Then I looked again at all the acts of oppression which were being done under the sun. And behold I saw the tears of the oppressed and that they had no one to comfort them; and on the side of their oppressors was power, but they had no one to comfort them.*

Preaching in Flin Flon

As our day to graduate and to leave for language school in Costa Rica approached we began to accept opportunities to share the vision. One of those trips took us to Flin Flon, Manitoba. I am not sure how long a drive it is but I do remember the drive. We left Regina in our Ford Granada in plenty of time. After about two hours, I realized my preaching clothes were still hung behind our front door. Preaching still felt new to me and I wanted everything to be perfect. I decided to turn back. When we finally left Regina the second time we barely had time for the drive and feared we might be late for our first meeting.

So I sped. I first saw the lights in the rear-view but then I heard the police siren. The RCMP (Royal Canadian Mounted Police) officer was unsympathetic. When I told him I was speeding to get to a church meeting on time he replied, "Speeding there is not setting a very good example." Thankfully my passengers did not talk about my bad example until hours later when I could see the humour in the situation.

Another time, we agreed to preach at three churches in one weekend. Not three times at one church, mind you, but in three different churches. Again, largely due to our unfamiliarity with distances on the prairies, we found out that we had almost agreed to mission impossible—speeding or not! We drove for two and a half hours to Saskatoon for the first meeting which was a Saturday afternoon church picnic. Afterwards we spent the night with friends. Next morning we drove to Kerrobert and arrived in time for a snack before I delivered the morning message in nearby Luseland and then drove to North Battleford. It was the last church on our list. I preached there in the evening.

Therein was the problem. North Battleford is a four and a half hour drive from Regina. Our boys had to attend school the next morning. After the evening service finished we left but it was 9:30 PM. It had been a hectic weekend and we were all exhausted. Neither Ann nor I knew precisely how long it would take to drive to Regina. An hour and a half later we arrived in Saskatoon and realized the earliest we could get home would be at 2 AM.

Fortunately the boys slept in the car and for them it was no problem. Ann was as tired as I, but she helped keep me awake. She woke up every twenty minutes and asked me how I was. I really fought my drooping eyes and my desire to sleep. I lost count of how many times I stopped the car and ran back and forth on the highway to let the cold revive me.

We never doubted that we both served Jesus but we were still unsure of whether we were eligible for mission work within our own church, so we continued to search for other groups. Ann tells the story best, *A Heritage of Miracles* written in 1995.

> *In the second year, God called us to missions and, surprisingly enough, even though God's call was in response to our prayers, it took a while to say yes. You see, by this time we had learned about District Operating Committee (DOM), Executive Operating Committee (EXCOM), District Superintendent (DS), Missionary Kid (MK), etc. and we loved our newly forming Alliance church roots although it was like learning a new language. We had also learned enough to know that we would have to leave the Alliance to follow God's calling—and that hurt even to think about. We struggled for months, then finally one day I said to Daddy, "It's Jesus who saved us; it's Jesus we must follow. And if we can't serve Him in the Alliance, then we'll have to leave. But if He wants us to stay, then He can cut through all the red tape and let us be Alliance missionaries. If God could knock down*

the walls of Jericho, He most certainly can cut through red tape!" So, we began to look into other mission agencies, and God's peace returned.

We hadn't got very far in our investigations when Arnold Cook came by. "Doug, if you will just calm down and wait awhile, there's a very good chance that you and Ann can go out as 'test case' missionaries with the Alliance." Test case meant that we had to show that older people could learn a new language and a new culture and adapt and serve. We were excited! We began to prepare. Daddy and I took Spanish at night school, and I made plans to study the next year at Canadian Theological Seminary (CTS).

That summer we went to Kelowna for Daddy's internship. It was so beautiful there! There was no assistant pastor there, and because Daddy was due to graduate in six months, there were various people who hoped Daddy would soon be the assistant pastor. One beautiful summer afternoon we were driving home from a visit in the hills. As I looked over this scenic valley, so perfect for raising a family, I said, "Lord, I'm weak. I'm vulnerable to the smoothness and softness of materialism. If you want us to be missionaries, you'd better move us along real quick!" In September, back in Regina, Daddy began making plans for his home service in January. Once again, Arnold Cook visited us. "Doug, you are al-

ways rushing things! Now, if you will just stay put in Regina and graduate in April like everyone else, it is a near certainty that you can leave in August as part of the contingent of Canadian Alliance missionaries." Daddy shouted "HALLELUJAH!" God indeed had answered and we were on our way! That year I studied, Daddy did his area study and we all got typhoid shots—ouch!

"God's will, will never lead you where His grace cannot sustain you." Never compromise—follow Him without reservation because God's sustaining grace is miraculous.

Yet another car miracle

Before we left Canada we sold the Granada and left it parked outside for the owners to pick up the next day. We left Regina for our overseas missionary work. That night the car was destroyed in a hit and run collision. The insurance paid us more than we had got from selling the car. So we gave the prospective purchasers a share of the difference. God wanted us to have more money and he wanted our friends to save their money! That is a miraculous provision, because it certainly isn't anything that man could plan.

Chile Chooses Us

The short answer is that God is sovereign and wanted us in Chile and specifically in Santiago for a work He had planned. God was looking for someone to say, "Here am I; send me."

Once we had been appointed as missionaries the process of being assigned started in earnest. We had our first meeting and were told that largely because of our age that we should not consider any Asian countries because of the difficulty of tonal languages. Who were we to argue? They suggested a Latin American country and asked us if we had a preference. Preference! I didn't even know how many countries there were in South America much less where they were located. Mainly in order not to appear to be stupid, I said, "Oh, any country will do. You decide." In addition to not revealing our lack of knowledge it seemed to be quite a spiritual reply.

We were assigned to Ecuador. That seemed fine to us as we knew our boys could go to school in Quito, Ecuador, and while we did not know which city we would be assigned to, at least we would all be in the same country.

I began to gather information for my field study—a main requirement for missionary candidates. Each missionary is expected to do a comprehensive study of the country he or she is assigned to before they leave.

The Mission's Board came a few weeks later and they asked if we would mind if they changed our designation to Peru. Evidently they had had numerous requests for Ecuador that year and they asked, "As you didn't ask for Ecuador, would you consider Peru?"

Those were the days of the Lima Encounter Program. Large churches were being built in the capital of Lima as a result of a revival. We were excited at this prospect and replied, "Yes."

The Mission's board members came back to us two weeks later and were very uncomfortable when they asked us to change destinations once again. "Would you consider going to Chile?"

Ann and I felt elated at the mention of Chile. It was like our spirits jumped within us. We knew nothing about Chile, including its location, yet it seemed that God really wanted us there and we rejoiced. We began to tell friends and family where we would be posted and I researched the field study to prepare us before we arrived in Chile.

This was one of a number of times in our lives that we relied heavily on the sovereignty of God. We didn't know what awaited us, we had no way of knowing, yet God was clearly in this so—we got excited.

SOUTH AMERICAN MISSIONS

An Ignominious Departure

The mission provided some guidelines for packing to move overseas but they seemed outdated and referred mostly to mosquito nets and storing goods in high humidity climates. We didn't know much about Chile but we weren't convinced that mosquito netting would be important.

We learned that missionaries packed in forty-five gallon steel drums and they should be welded shut to discourage theft. This paranoia persuaded us to put some small attractive items on the top of each drum in case someone broke in. We hoped it would encourage them to pick and run and leave the rest of the contents alone.

There were, no instructions about "how to pack" a forty-five gallon drum, so we improvised. Some things were self-evident, like packing the big items first and then fitting smaller ones around the bigger ones. I found out that a broom handle could push items down into crevices and almost make them disappear without apparently taking up any space at all. It was amazing how much stuff we fit into one barrel. Then came the *pièce de résistance.* As we packed in our basement and I saw the exposed floor joists above us it occurred to me that I could use a car jack to push down the lids so they were sealed prior to welding. In addition we did spot weld all the barrels. There were seven in total.

I now wonder what in the world we thought when we packed a king size water bed. It required a fair size crate made of plywood. The plywood crate alone weighed 80 pounds.

We had not traveled abroad except for the occasional foray across the U.S. border to shop. We had only flown within Western Canada and had no idea of the rigours of long-distance travel.

Our flight would leave from Toronto, so to see more of Canada we decided to travel to Toronto on the train. We thought, 'We will see something of this great country we are about to leave.'

The Snowsells assembled in the Regina Railway Station. Brandon and Colin were nine and ten years of age and very excited. We were to spend a year in Costa Rica and had packed everything we would need for a year in suitcases. We had six suitcases. The rest of our possessions, including the barrels, were to be shipped by sea. Via Rail was late and we sat in the station with a large number of other passengers who were also patiently waiting for the train.

We never heard an announcement for the arrival of the train, but there was suddenly the last call to board. We knew we had to be self- reliant, so I grabbed two bags, Ann two more and the boys struggled with one each. We rushed down the stairs to the tracks that were not visible from the waiting area. The rest of the passengers followed us. When we finally saw the train, we realized we were on the wrong side of the train!

All decorum, order and semblance of calm vanished. It was every man for himself. I shouted to the boys, "Follow me." We just reached the train seconds before it pulled out. I was amazed as we hauled ourselves into our car. We moved towards our seats when I realized that I hadn't seen Ann get on the train. I broke out in a cold sweat. "Stop the train! Stop the train! My wife has been left behind and we are on our way to Central America." The boys and I looked at Ann's empty seat and then caught sight of Ann running alongside the moving train. It might have been comical but at that moment I was shivering with fear.

I knew I couldn't stop the train but decided that we would get off at the next station and wait for the next train going west. I was sure there was nothing else I could do. We sat there feeling lower than we had ever felt in our lives. I thanked God that the boys were not crying. I was feeling extremely guilty and I was already imagining headlines: "Missionary wife lost as husband abandons her in train station."

I think we had all accepted that reality when Ann appeared led by a friendly conductor. He had seen Ann running beside the train and had reached down and pulled her up into the last car. He then accompanied her forward in the train until they found us. All's well that ends well, but I was badly shaken.

The trip itself was all we had imagined. No one can appreciate the size of this great county until they have journeyed across it. It is awe-inspiring and we enjoyed it.

In Toronto we stayed for several days at the Cook's home. It was a time for a last-minute orientation, a farewell to friends and resting for the next leg of our journey that would take us to Costa Rica via Miami.

We were traveling with friends and missionary colleagues, Ken and Vicki and their four children. We thought that *we* had a huge amount of luggage! We were fortunate that Arnold Cook had vast travel experience. He ensured we arrived at the airport in plenty of time. Nowadays, travelers are expected to arrive a couple of hours before an international flight. We arrived three hours before departure when that was not a general rule. Our part of the terminal was empty. No check-in attendants had arrived.

We were first in line! The airline charged us a huge amount for overweight luggage. Fortunately Arnold had his credit card. Then Ken and Vicki's turn came. The agent said, "That box is too big, sir." Ken replied, "No, it isn't, I checked the manual carefully and it is OK." Unfortunately that was not the best answer.

"You," said the agent pointing to the six of them, "Move over to that line." They waited until all the other passengers had been processed before the ticket agent dealt with them. In the meantime we moved through security and customs and went into the boarding lounge. We sat there and wondered if we should abandon our friends and board the plane or whether we should wait.

We waited until the final boarding call when the six of them, wild-eyed, ran into the boarding lounge. They were frazzled, but none the worse for wear. We all gratefully boarded the plane. We must have been a sight. There were ten of us. Our recent panic flashed in our eyes and we staggered onto the plane carrying the maximum allowable hand baggage.

I reminded myself this was just the first leg of our journey. My sons asked, "Dad, are we having an adventure?" I replied, "Yes."

I knew that eventually we would face a language barrier but I didn't expect it at Miami. When we stepped off our Air Canada flight I felt that we had landed in Latin America. The main language in Miami airport is Spanish. Flight announcements came first in Spanish, then in

Spanglish, which is English we could not understand because of the heavy accent.

We didn't have to check any bags as they had been checked through to San Jose. We had time to fill before our next flight. I was in shock and virtually commanded my family not to wander and insisted that we find the boarding lounge for our next flight. Our colleagues however, meant to use the time in other ways.

Theirs might not have been the wisest choice in retrospect. As the time came nearer to board and the first invitation to do so was made—at least we guessed that was what they were saying—there was still no sign of the traveling companions. Déjà vu, all over again. As before, we sat and considered if we would go down with the ship or climb aboard let them, women and children included fend for themselves. We quickly decided that we were not heroes and began to board, just as they again swooped into view in full flight, hand baggage trailing behind.

This at least had been much smoother than our departure from Toronto. Still, the language barrier was suffocating. We couldn't understand anything as now no English was spoken. I sat with one of the boys behind my wife and my other son thinking back on the process that had led up to this flight. Had I been a bank manager only five years earlier? Had we not lived in considerable security in our recently constructed home in Surrey, B.C., only seven years previously? I looked out the window of the plane. It was a particularly beautiful day and from our altitude we could see the entire island of Cuba. These were days of high tension between Cuba and the free world. Once again cold panic overwhelmed me. What had I done to my family? What was I doing? O God, forgive me.

A Year in Costa Rica

We are here! We are really here. We have no return ticket. We don't know anyone. Few speak English and none of us understand a word of Spanish. We follow the crowd, they will lead us. "*Proximo,*" says a man in uniform. We don't understand so he motions us forward. We present our passports. He looks, realizes he can't communicate with us, stamps the passport and motions us through.

Now we have to find our stack of baggage. Again, we follow the crowd. Then, finally we see a friendly North American face holding up a sign for us. We have found a saviour. Again, if only for a moment, the language barrier is broken. We are met by two people who have been sent to pick us up. As our entourage will not fit into anything smaller than a bus, we all climb into a small van and pack it to the top with our bags. We ask ourselves why we have brought all this stuff, and then answer, "because we are going to be here for a year."

Everything is new. Our senses struggle to keep up. Are those all palm trees? What are those other large-leaf trees? What are the small bushes that grow out of the roots of the banana trees? Why are the houses surrounded with high fences? Are those houses? They are made of corrugated iron sheets that are completely rusted out. In Canada they would be consigned to the dump.

Colin stares out the window of the van and looks aghast. Clusters of rusted buildings appear to lean in defiance of gravity. They look like playing-card houses but made of corrugated iron sheets. He asks, "Are we going to live in one of those?"

"Good question, son. I don't think so," I say, but even I am not convinced. We actually didn't find out for a few days where we would stay as we were temporarily billeted with another missionary family. They lived above a grocery store.

The location turned out to be a mixed blessing; groceries were always close at hand, but the smells that wafted upstairs just about gagged us. The rules of hygiene were almost unknown to the locals. Milk was delivered in plastic bags and often left on the street in the tropical heat where it turned bad. It was then poured away into the gutter.

The next day we were shown our new home, but it wasn't yet ready for us. It was in a new subdivision opposite a park. It could not have been nicer and we thanked our missionary colleagues who had secured it for us.

Now we began our introduction to another culture in earnest. We were told that we were to have a maid and were introduced to Amable. She proved as friendly as her name. She cooked and cleaned and that left us to dedicate our energy to learning Spanish.

Electrical Hook-up

We had a couple of weeks of free electricity when we moved as the electrical installation did not have a meter. That was fine but did not last long. I recall the afternoon when two young men arrived to hook up the meter.

We were given an object lesson on the difference between safety standards in Canada and Costa Rica. As it was afternoon it was pouring rain, as usual. We were safe and dry inside the house. I noticed that neither of these young men had hard hat, gloves or any safety equipment and were dressed in sandals, slacks, and t-shirts. Up went the one man to connect to the meter box on the side of the house. So far he had not yet touched any live wires. Next he moved the ladder to the power pole. I saw that the ladder just leaned up against the electric pole. It tottered and moved about. Both of them were sopping wet and, as one of them reached for the live wires, I hastily asked my boys to move away from the window. I expected to see a huge blue spark followed by two flying bodies. The electrical circuits in Costa Rica are 220 volts, not the usual 110 volts to which we were accustomed in North America. But they safely installed the meter.

We also met Rodolfo. He was a young man hired by the community as a guard. We soon learned that all windows had bars and entrances had two doors, one of them made of steel bars. Most neighbourhoods employed guards or things would disappear!

Rodolfo was not much older than our own boys, but we quickly established a rapport over soccer, despite the language barrier. We also had a television and once Rodolfo realized he was a welcome guest, he spent a lot of time at our place.

One Sunday morning Rodolfo came over early to watch a game. We were busy preparing to leave for church. I sensed that Rodolfo wanted to ask us about our faith. He was Catholic and knew we held slightly different beliefs, but I was impatient to get to church and brushed him off. I didn't want to be late for church.

The rest of that morning God and my conscience assailed me. I wondered what kind of Christian was I that I did not make time to talk with someone who wanted to know more about God?

We were back home by early afternoon and thankfully Rodolfo soon appeared. I then had the privilege of leading my first "Latino" to a saving knowledge of Jesus Christ. It was strange because I didn't speak Spanish. But, I have learned a vital principle, "if you are willing, God is able."

I have always memorized key parts of scripture. Numbers are the same in Spanish and English. Therefore, as I knew the biblical references, I walked Rodolfo through the parts of the Spanish Bible that explained sin, forgiveness and acceptance of Christ. Most of it was accomplished by pointing and with gestures but his tears told me he understood the eternal story. I prayed for him in English and I am sure God translated for his ears.

Eternal Spring

The climate in San Jose has been described as eternal spring. For us Canadians it felt more like eternal summer. The temperature varied little during the year and the change of seasons was noted only by the change between dry and rainy seasons. After we had been there for some months, I could wake the family and announce, "Today's weather will be clear and sunny this morning with temperatures reaching 23 degrees Celsius. Rain is probable around 2:30 PM and there will be sun and heat later in the afternoon." I could make this forecast with a ninety percent chance of accuracy on any day. My family started to yearn for seasons and for changes in daylight, and even for snow.

There were eighteen in our denomination who were all in Costa Rica to learn Spanish. We were encouraged to mingle with Costa Ricans, or Ticos as they are called.

We were advised not to attend the same church, but to spread ourselves into the community. We chose a church called *La Colina* that was two bus rides away. We chose it from a list of names without visiting the church. We were shyly greeted at the door but quickly received a warm welcome. It seemed unimportant that we couldn't converse directly. After the first hour, when we did not understand anything in the service, we were quite depressed, especially as services were two hours long, but then God rescued us because we all knew the next chorus and we all sang quite heartily in English. I realized that our God and their God was the same. He understood our discomfort and comforted us all.

The offering came by, and I noticed they took particular care to see that it was passed to each of us. Even among the average Protestant churches of Costa Rica, ours stood out in its poverty. There was not a complete floor in the building and the hard benches were two by fours with no back rests. People stood in the dirt.

They couldn't afford instruments in the church so they clapped hands and sung with their beautiful voices and worshipped God. Stars of the congregation were those who had guitars. We had one super star with an electric guitar but unfortunately he didn't know how to play it! Often the worship leader would start a chorus and expect our "guitarist" to pick up the tune, but too often the guitarist would turn his back and tune his guitar because he didn't

Douglas enjoying the local fruit

know the chorus. He couldn't tune his guitar well, either, but sometimes he would break forth in the only song he knew, but nobody else in the congregation knew what he was trying to play. I gained a new appreciation for those who lead worship well.

To help us learn Spanish we were encouraged to shop at the outdoor markets. There was one just a bus ride away from where we lived, although we had quite a walk to the bus stop. We took our rattan shopping bags for the produce we'd buy.

"You can be a shopper in any language" is an aphorism we found to be very true. The vendors bend over backward to help you spend your money. Frequently we negotiated our purchases on paper, but once we learned the value of *sucres* (Costa Rican currency) in Canadian dollars and realized we could purchase enough fresh fruit and vegetables to feed our family for a month, and at a cost of just twenty dollars, we went wild.

We didn't see why we should buy just a few bananas when we could afford to purchase a whole stalk of the deliciously sweet *datils*. And so we bought oranges, pineapples, carrots and onions and almost anything we desired—except apples. When we had to go home we managed to each get two bags into the bus. But when the bus dropped us at our stop we faced more than a "short walk" to our house. We had to stop several times for rests. Our arms were nearly torn from their sockets by the time we arrived at our front door. The short walk that earlier had taken fifteen minutes became nearly an hour-long hike.

Language School Before Chile

Our language school was in the suburb of *Tres Rios* and over its large gated archway was inscribed the words, "Spanish is the only language spoken here."

We learned abstract nouns, adjectives, and different verb tenses. We had to understand what was said in Spanish—because Spanish was the only language spoken. The teachers were great. Our favourite was Elizabet, a grammar teacher, who communicated really well. Sometimes I forgot she was speaking a foreign language because I understood so easily what she taught.

We were among three hundred international students, but the classes were kept very small with only six or seven in each. After two weeks we were all evaluated and put in classes according to our progress. I was quite disappointed to see that I was in one of the lowest of the forty groups.

I did not appear to progress because I remained within the lowest of the groups, yet I knew I was working hard. I had an inspired work ethic that I'd learned from my years in bank management. I recognized my handicap of being older than most students, but with hard work and discipline, I was determined to make up for this deficiency. I was arrogant, but God was going to teach me a lesson.

I knew that all our church students would face an oral exam at the end of the first year. I had heard that if you failed you were sent home. As the date for my examination approached and my Spanish did not improve, I became terrified.

Ann and I wondered what we would ever say to all those faithful people from Canada who had prayed and given us support. We thought that at less than a year we might have the shortest missionary career on record

After nearly six months, with classes five days a week, my Spanish was barely rudimentary. In the markets I could barely distinguish between "*si*" and "*no*." I regularly got up at 4AM. to hit the books. I had practiced incessantly on the street but the results were often comical. I remember an incident in a local camera store where I was well known. I said to the young girl behind the counter, "*Es muy lindo hoy.*" She turned beet red and I knew I had blown it. I meant to say it was a nice day, but realized later that I had said that she was very pretty today. What the young girl heard was not what I intended to say and neither of us knew how to exit this embarrassing moment.

My inability to converse in Spanish caused me all kinds of difficulties with my pride. I remember being cheated at the grocery store over change because although I knew what the money was worth, the cashier took advantage of me, knowing I couldn't defend myself.

I had trouble with taxis too. In Costa Rica drivers rarely use their meters and don't depend on street signs but rely on local landmarks. Our home was `on the street 50 meters west of the gas station and 300 meters south of it', even though the gas station hadn't been there for years. When you get a cab, you negotiate with the driver by telling him where you want to go and haggle over the fare. Although I wasn't an expert haggler, I did prevent us from being gouged.

One evening, after an open house at our sons' school, we decided to take a taxi home as it was raining. I tried to negotiate a fixed rate with a cab driver and told him where we needed to go. He just couldn't understand me and I'm not sure I could have made sense of the Spanish I tried to speak. He sadly shook his head and couldn't take us. Ann and I ended up walking home in the rain and the dark. I was humiliated.

I became very depressed. It seemed that my

Spanish was no better after six months than it had been after a week. But the oral exam, which I had to pass, was approaching fast. The date for the exam had been set.

One morning a few weeks before the dreaded oral exam I arose at my usual 4 AM., went to my study desk and sat down. I wondered, "What is the use?" I sat quietly. This was God's moment. I heard His still small voice in the morning darkness. "Doug, have you forgotten something?" I knew instantly what He meant. I had chosen as my life's verse Mathew 6:33, which says, "*But seek first His kingdom and His righteousness, and all these things will be added to you.*" I broke down and wept at my arrogance and my stupidity. I realized how quickly I had abandoned my own principles and my God.

I folded my Spanish book and opened the only book that mattered to me, the Bible. We had a sweet reunion and I enjoyed the renewed fellowship with my faithful Lord. He had never left me, but I needed to return to my senses.

I also continued my Spanish work. I studied and practiced but never again did I forsake my Lord. He had my attention and He had first place.

Three weeks later the latest results were posted in the language school. I looked for my name at the bottom of the groups but it wasn't there. I finally found it in the top ten. Alone and with six months of hard work I had not progressed with Spanish, but God had helped me to accomplish His will in just a month.

I completed my year at language school in the top five groups and thank Jesus.

Tamarindo Rip Tide

We enjoyed two brief holidays during our year of language study. The most memorable time was a long weekend at the magnificent Tamarindo Resort.

The Costa Rican currency, the *sucre*, was for a time seriously devalued against the US dollar. For a few months, we who got our money in US dollars were in an enviable position.

As I planned our family break, I realized that we could fly from San Jose, spend three nights in air conditioned cabins at the three-star resort and eat at the resort restaurant and it would only cost sixty dollars per person. Our purchasing power had increased exponentially.

Gorgeous does not describe the hotel and its grounds. Located on the blue Pacific, our cabins were 250 yards back off the beach, partially hidden by huge coconut palms. There was an enormous freshwater pool with direct access to the equally large outdoor restaurant. We ate our meals under an immense artificial thatched roof with a 360 degree view. The ocean itself was South Pacific blue and around 85 degrees Fahrenheit.

I am not fond of swimming. I have a quick dip on a hot day but don't linger in the water. Here, I was fascinated by the empty, clean beach on which it was too hot to sit. So I went in the water. I tried body surfing, something I had never done before.

I was swimming with a colleague and we ventured out of the shallows to find bigger waves. After forty-five minutes I looked back to the beach. I realized we were catching waves that should have carried us closer to the shore, but in reality were going farther and farther out. I told my friend.

We tried to swim towards shore, but panicked as we realized that by swimming very strongly we merely stayed put. The beach remained quite a way off. To our right was a rock breakwater jutting out from shore. Our only hope was to swim there before the rip tide pulled us out. For twenty minutes we swam parallel to the beach hoping to reach those rocks. Eventually we made the breakwater.

We were exhausted. Our adrenaline had probably saved our lives. Thankfully we had done the right thing by swimming across rather than fighting the current.

Central Market

One of my favourite places in San Jose was the Mercado Central. Once we established our walking patterns I started to buy all our fruit and vegetables there. It was under cover and open most of the time. The nearby markets were only open on certain days.

I befriended a fruit vender called Luis. He was an entrepreneur and a free spirit. He even invited us to meet his family. His beautiful wife, Jasmine, and daughter greeted us with the same warmth as Luis. In our year in Costa Rica Luis introduced me to numerous new tropical fruits.

I thought I knew a lot but realized I knew very little about the most common tropical fruits. When I purchased a pineapple, he asked, "What kind?" Our family fell in love with a little sweet Costa Rican pineapple called Amarillo. We all loved its yellow flesh and it was incredibly sweet. It was like eating brown sugar. Papayas were soon a breakfast staple in our house. They were huge and we learned to eat them with lime juice. There were *granadillas* and *guayaba* and others that I now only recognize when I see them because I have forgotten their names.

One of the lessons our family faced was how to deal with all the poverty. On Sundays after church, we would eat at McDonalds. Our boys became very conscious of the young kids who crowded up to the windows to watch us. We gave our sons their allowances in very small coins and they often gave away their entire allowance before we got to church!

Graduation

We left Costa Rica in August 1982. When we arrived we had suffered from heat and slept under sheets but by the time we left we were quite comfortable sleeping under two blankets. We had settled in well. However, our family was under a pall because we'd have to part from our sons in Quito at the Alliance Academy. It would be their home for the next few years.

We stayed with them in Ecuador for two weeks and helped them settle in, personalize their rooms and explore Quito. Later, some Chileans couldn't understand how we could bear to be separated from our children. They thought we had different hearts or were just incredibly cruel. If they had witnessed our last family prayer before we left our sons they would have not have thought that way.

We gathered in a football huddle in Brandon's room. My recollection is blurry and fogged with tears but I recall crying out to God and demanding that He hear my plea, "Father, we may never again be a normal family. I beg you to keep us a united family even though we are separated by hundreds of miles."

Ann and I believe that God honoured my request. In fact we share something that perhaps only missionaries share—the indescribable joy of being together again.

The first time the boys came to Chile was at Christmas. We put all our mattresses on our bedroom floor and talked until the dawn light was in the sky. When we went to sleep we all snuggled on the floor.

The farewells were never easy. One time at Santiago Airport we were there with another missionary family. We all stood paralyzed on the observation deck and watched the plane disappear into the haze. We asked the other family—they had raised five children in Chile and had been in the country for thirty seven years—"Does it get any easier?" They replied tearfully, "No."

Extract from Douglas Snowsell's next book

A LIFETIME IN TEN DAYS AND TEN YEARS

Arriving in Chile and then Bolivia

We left Costa Rica and stopped for three weeks in La Paz, Bolivia, on our way to Chile. A good friend of ours lived there and had recently witnessed the death of one friend and the serious injury of another. We hoped our visit would lift his spirits.

Bolivia's La Paz airport is 11,000 feet above sea level. By way of comparison, oxygen masks deploy in an aircraft if it loses compression when flying higher 10,000 feet. Our aircraft landed and parked a considerable distance from the terminal. It seemed at the time to be a conspiracy designed to make the gringo pant. We didn't appreciate it because we were not traveling light. We each struggled with two carry-on bags that weighed twenty pounds.

We came down the aircraft stairs onto blistering tarmac strip and were herded like sheep towards the terminal that was over 400 feet away. I had only made it halfway when I felt my heart pound severely hard and it nearly jumped out of my throat. When we finally reached the terminal we had to wait and I had time to recover. I understood, with my limited Spanish, that the bags were being brought from the plane.

The bags appeared a few at a time and passengers claimed their bags and went to customs. I got restless and quite anxious when our bags did not appear. I was not sure I had properly understood so I ducked under a restricted area sign and looked out onto the tarmac. Two men had our suitcases open and were rifling through them. I shouted, "What are you doing?" They didn't challenge that I was in a restricted area but hastily put stuff back and we were quickly called for our turn through customs. It was quite a welcome to a new country.

Our friend, Charlie picked us up and saw we were a little traumatized. We drove down a winding road into La Paz which is still 10,000 feet above sea level. It was barely 6 PM but it was already growing dark. Ann and I were hungry, tired and in shock from the day's events, which included saying goodbye to our boys. While we waited for the meal, Charlie made us some cocaine tea. It was a strange welcome to Bolivia. Actually, I believe that God in His great wisdom provides the cocaine plant as it permits people to live comfortably at these high altitudes. Unfortunately, mankind has also found out how to corrupt its use. We drank this rather bitter multipurpose brew and it both calmed our stomachs and warmed us at the same time.

A simple supper of hearty soup was put on the table. Charlie explained we should eat immediately and not wait for the others to be served. At this altitude food cools very rapidly—less than five minutes between near boiling to being unpleasantly cool.

The meal did us good and even though we were tired we wanted to catch up with what had been happening in Charlie's life. We retired to the sitting room. Charlie immediately prepared to light the fire. He put wood in the grate without either kindling or paper. He was my host so I said nothing and held my tongue. It turns out we were in for an education.

Charlie went into the car port and drained off about a half liter of gasoline from a jerry can. I knew Charlie was a sensible man and made little of it until I saw him pour the gasoline over the wood. I was uncomfortable and felt my panic rise. I wondered what kind of place this was where the officials had tried to rob me and now my friend appeared to have little regard for his life.

I moved towards the kitchen because I could easily escape to the outside. I barely listened to Charlie's explanation, "Don't worry, gasoline burns differently up here." In went a lit match. I had one foot in the doorway and was ready to run but I watched an amazing thing. Instead of creating an explosion that I had expected would blow the chimney right off the house, the gasoline burned like a soft blue-flamed candle. We were soon warm and cozy.

Bolivia is a country of stunning contrasts. In the centre of town are several four star hotels in which drug lords frolic and live, but surrounding these hotels are miles and miles of squalor. People can barely earn enough to feed themselves and their families. Charlie told of us of one of the main employers, a mine where for decades men had descended into the centre of the earth to extract tin. In the mine's earlier years the Spanish conquistadores used the Incas in forced labour because they could work hard at that altitude. The Spaniards had an exploitative mentality and thought the Incas expendable. They worked them until they died. The narrow spiral stairs that were used before mechanization remain as do the grottos where sacrifices were left by the miners for the gods of the mountain.

The oppression and sadness we witnessed in the populace was almost unbearable. Few people smiled and they all walked with bowed heads. The people seemed suspicious because they had been raised never to expect anything without being exploited.

My friend and two other young men had dedicated themselves to live and work in this environment to bring the message of hope in Jesus Christ.

Just a few months before our arrival, these two young Latino men had been preparing for Bolivia's annual liberation day. The day is always celebrated with a lot of firecrackers. Most people make the larger ones themselves. They are so big; we in the West might call them bombs! The two young men were in the kitchen, making their "cherry bombs" on the table. Charlie was working on his computer in another room. Suddenly there was an explosion. One of the young men was killed outright and the other was seriously wounded up his left side where it had been exposed above the table.

Charlie saw a horrible gory sight of blood and there were body parts strewn everywhere. Body parts had even stuck to the walls. Instinctively he threw the corpse in the back of their pickup and put his injured friend in the passenger seat and drove to hospital. Luckily his friend's life was saved, but his left eye and hand were not so lucky. Then most unexpectedly, Charlie was arrested by the secret police and charged with terrorism.

Prisons in South America are bad but to fall into the hands of the secret police is often fatal. Charlie was held in a dark cell several floors below street level and kept in solitary confinement for six days. He did not know if he would live or die. With the help of a diplomatic friend, he was eventually released. However, he was so traumatized after his release he would not walk on the sidewalk in front of the building when he took us to see where it had happened.

Our time in Bolivia was not all bad, quite the contrary. Although we did not know the significance of it at the time, we met Ofelia and Mario and their family in La Paz. This "chance" meeting would be of great importance to the work we were to do in Chile.

Charlie also arranged an outing to Lake Titicaca. We were extremely excited to visit the highest inhabited lake in the world. A guide was hired to drive us there and back. He arrived very early one morning. By 6AM we were driving out of La Paz up to the Alto Plano where the airport is located.

While we drove in the city we were not unduly alarmed except that our driver ignored red lights and stop signs and thought them only relevant in the case of an accident.

However, as we exceeded 50 kilometers an hour on the road out of the city, the front end of our VW pickup shook violently. We realised it was going to be an extraordinarily long day, especially if a wheel fell off.

We had planned to get to the lake before noon but we didn't arrive until early afternoon. Our trip continued on to the lake where another guide took us out to La Isla del Sol which is supposed to be the last stronghold of the Incas in their war with the Spanish.

At this high altitude all combustion engines lose power due to the lack of oxygen. Our little launch was powered by a 35 HP Evinrude that at lower altitude would have skimmed along. As it was, we might have gone faster if we had all rowed. On the return trip the boat driver kept nodding off and veering off course, which wasted even more time.

We got back to our whiz mobile and were prepared for the drive back to La Paz. It was already getting dark. Our trip home involved a short ferry trip to avoid a much longer way by road.

The "ferry" was comprised several logs tied together with planks across them for a maximum two-vehicle load. I was not looking forward to this crossing in the dark. It was dark and the ferry had stopped running at dusk. Our driver wasn't fazed and flashed his lights to get the attention of the boatman on the far shore. We were parked in front of a tavern but only became aware when a pair of men stumbled out on the street to continue a fight they had started inside. Their fight attracted a crowd who scrutinised us very carefully and made us feel quite uncomfortable.

Our driver made contact with his blinking headlights and announced the ferry was on its way. Our driver and boatman were soon arguing over the "fare." The boatman held that as it was after hours a special rate applied. The driver just as adamantly claimed that he had paid the fare on the way over and it included the return trip. We watched the bar fight while our driver and the boatman haggled until an agreement was reached. Then we drove on to the ferry. The night was black as oil. I wondered how long it would take just to find our bodies if this flimsy log ferry sank.

Once we landed on the other side, I thought we would drive uneventfully home, but I hadn't allowed for the unexpected. Just after we left the ferry we drove up into a mini pass—a shallow cut with banks on each side. Then in the headlights we saw a family blocking the road. Bandits are not unheard of and we quickly locked the doors. Our driver, who could speak Quechewa, learned that one of the family was sick and they had to go to La Paz for medicine.

All eight of them wanted to go. We convinced them we could only take two. It all sounded reasonable and I started to make room in the cab. I thought one would sit in the front and the other in the back. At this altitude it was bitter cold outside. Charlie quickly brought me back to reality. "Doug, these folks probably haven't ever taken a real bath. We will all gag from the smell."

So these two rode in the back of an open pickup. They seemed to take the cold okay but I think I would have let my dog up front.

Our three-week stay passed very quickly but we made tentative plans for Charlie to visit us in Chile before we left. Our time had ended but unexpected events continued. There was a general strike the day we left and the road to the airport was strewn with rocks. Some rocks were still being added as we passed! We trusted that Charlie would be alright by himself.

Author Biography

Douglas Snowsell was born and raised in Kelowna B.C. and is part of a third generation orchardist family.

After the death of his father he left farming and, almost inadvertantly, became a successful banker.

At age 34, he took an unexpected turn and entered a Bible seminary. After he successfully graduated he and his wife Ann took their young family to South America and began a second career in the ministry.

During his sixteen-year career as a missionary for the Christian & Missionary Alliance, Doug Snowsell pioneered a modern approach to urban Latin church growth, first in Santiago, Chile and later in Madrid, Spain. Douglas Snowsell lives in Victoria, B.C., where he is still involved in growth, although principally of the vegetable variety.